CHARACTER *at* WORK

CHARACTER *at* WORK

BUILDING PROSPERITY THROUGH THE PRACTICE OF VIRTUE

WILLIAM J. O'BRIEN

Foreword by

PETER M. SENGE

Paulist Press
New York/Mahwah, NJ

Library of Congress Cataloging-in-Publication Data

O'Brien, William J., d. 2002.
  Character at work : building prosperity through the practice of virtue / William J. O'Brien.
    p. cm.
  ISBN 978-0-8091-4588-1 (alk. paper)
  1. Corporate culture--Moral and ethical aspects. 2. Leadership--Moral and ethical aspects. 3. Moral development. 4. Business ethics. 5. Success in business--Moral and ethical aspects. I. Title.

  HD58.7.O224 2008
  174'.4--dc22
                                        2008026106

Published by Paulist Press
997 Macarthur Boulevard
Mahwah, New Jersey 07430

www.paulistpress.com

Printed and bound in the
United States of America

CONTENTS

FOREWORD

Not long ago, an executive from one of the largest corporations in the world showed a group of us at a meeting the "corporate values" tee shirt he had recently acquired. On the back were the corporation's values: integrity, respect, communication, openness. On the front was the corporation's name: Enron.

The first question many people will have with regard to this book will probably be: "Why should I read a book written by a CEO who passed away six years ago, whom I have never heard of, and whose company I have never heard of? An insurance company!"

All I can say in response is: "What will keep your company from being the next Enron?"

What company today does not have a "values statement"? In how many would the CEO be fired because he or she violates those values? In how many would a front-line person be able to come forward and share with management violations of the company's values, without potentially putting his or her career at risk? How many companies have worked seriously to build the capacity to confront and learn from gaps between what is espoused and what is practiced? Yet that is exactly what any company serious about values must do. After all, none of us are saints. The real purpose of articulating corporate values is so that we can discover gaps between our values and our actions and learn from them. The fact that so few companies even take such capacity-building seriously suggests that they are more interested in espousing rather than living their values.

This is but one lesson I learned from Bill O'Brien, who was one of my true mentors. I can honestly say that there is no businessperson from whom I have learned more.

Bill served as architect of one of the most dramatic, sustained corporate revivals I know of, first as Marketing Vice President and then as CEO. In 1970, Hanover Insurance was, for all intents and purposes, bankrupt. In 1990, an independent study by McKinsey of the U.S. property and liability insurance industry placed Hanover in the top quartile of the industry in profitability and growth for the decade of the 1980s. It was the only company that was so ranked which had not been in the top quartile in the 1970s. This dramatic turnaround was accomplished with no major acquisitions to fuel growth, and with what most in the industry would regard as a critical strategic liability, independent agents. In other words, Hanover found a way to generate growth internally and relied on people who were not its employees to sell its product—people who could also sell competitors' products.

Interestingly, Bill and his predecessor as CEO, Jack Adam, regarded independent agents as an asset rather than a liability. It seemed to them that people who were not your employees had freedom to do what they felt was best, rather than being compromised by what the boss wanted. If you created aims and a way of working that they truly valued, they would volunteer their support and commitment. If you gave them another story that smelled of "corporate BS," they would defect. Hanover's structure of independent agents, Adam and O'Brien reasoned, was the perfect setting to see if they could develop a set of guiding ideas and practices that truly treated customers and those who serve customers fairly. Voluntarism for people at the front lines, they believed, was the surest path toward integrity. So, way before people thought about "network organizations," "strategic alliances," and other voluntary affiliations to grow enterprises, O'Brien and Hanover were creating them.

Likewise, with innovations in many other areas, O'Brien and his Hanover colleagues ventured where few predecessors had gone. They worked to develop a "values-based, vision-driven" organization well before writing values and vision statements became a corporate fad. They identified knowledge generation and diffusion—organizational learning—as a core source of competitive advantage before anyone had written about "knowledge management." Along with a few other pioneers such as VISA, Hanover developed a radical, decentralized governance system, with divisions reporting to independent internal boards, before people ever talked about "decentering" large corporations.

In brief, the main reasons you may not have heard of Hanover is that it was so far ahead of its time that few knew about or understood what O'Brien and his cohorts were doing.

I knew about Hanover because, in 1980, Bill joined a group of CEOs that met regularly at MIT to talk about deep changes that were starting to play out in the business world. The group included Ray Stata, CEO of Analog Devices and founder of the Massachusetts High Technology Council, and Arie de Geus of Shell, from whom we all learned about organizational learning for the first time. This CEO group became a prime incubator for many of the ideas that eventually came to underpin work on organizational learning, and the collaboration among the companies established the pattern that evolved eventually into the SoL (Society for Organizational Learning) global network.

From the outset, it was clear that Bill was a distinctive contributor among this group of leaders. His remarkable gifts for simply articulating complex issues and seeing to the bottom of things became deeply appreciated, as did his resolute unwillingness to swim with the tide of management fad and fashion.

For example, early in our meetings, he spoke of the importance of developing a "home-grown philosophy" in an organization. This had nothing to do with being closed to outside influences and developments in the larger world. Indeed, O'Brien was famous within Hanover for continually rocking the boat of organization tradition by bringing in people and ideas from outside. But he was equally adamant that no real change could start to occur unless new ideas were internalized and eventually became a transparent part of the organization's own way of doing things. In this way, he was able to help the organization achieve balance between change and continuity, to keep experimenting without getting caught up in the "flavor of the month" programitis that afflicts so many corporations. "You must be truthful to the roots of the company," Bill says—"transplants will be rejected." The only way Bill believed a company could "sustain continual radical innovation yet not chase fads is to have theory and practice rooted in your soul."

Theory is a word you rarely hear from managers. For O'Brien it was crucial. "One day," he says, "I was reading a twenty-year-old memo. What it said was exactly what people were saying all around me at that very time. Every six to ten years, the insurance industry cycle shifts. When this happens, there are predictable patterns. When business gets hard, people withdraw authority from the field, cut the bottom ten to twenty percent of their agents, and publish new rules for more stringent underwriting and cost containment. Six to ten years later, when business booms, all of this is reversed. The essence of the type of manager we wanted to develop was someone who could confront current problems with an appreciation of history, someone who would not accept solutions with negative long-term consequences. When you do that, you not only jeopardize your business, you demoralize your people."

Bill's interest in theory extended from the theory of the business to the theory of building a values-based organization. In the 1970s, Adam and O'Brien jointly developed three guiding values: localness (make no decision at a higher or more central level that could be competently made more locally), openness (encourage people at all levels to challenge the assumptions underlying their and others' decisions), and merit (the ultimate criterion for all decisions is the health of the enterprise as a whole). Clarifying these three values took an entire decade—it took that long to discover what values were really needed to guide decisions, and to develop shared understanding of what these values meant in practice. Gradually, Hanover's board of directors started to understand the importance of these values as well, but they were puzzled by O'Brien's approach to building commitment. He began to get pressure from the board to put these values into the performance review process, as many companies were starting to do. "Only if you make people's promotions and pay depend on living according to our values can you show people in the organization that you are really serious," board members would say. "Thank God, we never caved in to this pressure," says O'Brien. What the board members had to come to understand, O'Brien says, "is that a value is only a value when it is voluntarily chosen."

Incisiveness like this gradually led to Bill being recognized among many peers as a "philosopher-CEO" extraordinaire. After he retired, he became a personal advisor to several CEOs attempting to bring about similar transformations in corporate culture. When he would make one of his rare visits to one of these companies, it was quite an occasion. "People value Bill's counsel so much," commented one executive. "He has become a genuine elder in the SoL community."

In 1998, we were launching a new SoL research initiative on the challenges of assessing business performance in ways that deepen and extend innovation rather than intimidating people and reinforcing fear and internal competition. Bill opened this session with a presentation that was vintage O'Brien, on "my nine frustrations as a CEO":

1) **Fog in seeing real business results.**
   It is very difficult to see how a business is performing in fewer than five to ten years, given the inherent ebbs and flows in any business.

2) **We don't understand gestation periods.**
   It is difficult to judge the effectiveness of basic innovations in culture, processes, and capabilities, given inherent time delays.

3) **War between the short term and the long term.**
   People at the front lines often know that disinvestment is occurring in a business, but this can be covered up for many years.

4) **Self-scorekeeping: Is it more temptation than management can handle?**

   Pressures to make short-term results look good are especially pernicious, given that companies are basically their own scorekeepers.

5) **Is the basic problem lack of knowledge or lack of virtue?**

6) **How do we embed "leanness" as a basic virtue, starting at the top?**

   The temptation is to get "fat" in good times, which leads to large-scale layoffs. "I worry about companies that can lay off one thousand people but not one person in a position of authority who fails to command people's respect."

7) **Much damage is done trying to quantify what should not be quantified.**

8) **Much improvement is possible by simply avoiding dumb things that everyone says you must do.**

9) **What does it take to develop a "legacy mentality" in corporations?**

   A core leadership dilemma today arises because those at the top want to "put their stamp" on the organization, thereby leading to superficial versus significant changes, which require longer time-horizons than "one CEO's watch."

It is impossible to read this list today and not be struck by O'Brien's remarkable prescience. For example, his fourth, fifth, and sixth points capture succinctly the essence of the current hand-wringing about corporate accounting practices. I remember Bill speaking that evening about the inevitable dilemmas that develop within large accounting firms: on the one hand, auditors are responsible for conducting impartial audits of client companies, and on the other hand, they are under enormous internal pressures to "not lose a key client."

As O'Brien pointed out then, the core problem is a system of self-scorekeeping, rather than the failings of any one individual firm, in an environment that gives little attention to cultivating virtue. As he told his board many years ago, this is not something that can be done by fiat or by rules from the top. It is a matter of creating an environment for genuine maturation, starting with the model set by those in positions of power. If people in the most senior and visible positions do not cultivate virtue, no set of rules will ever compensate.

Which brings us to this book.

In a sense, this is an old-fashioned book. In many ways, the connection between leadership and wisdom represents the oldest thread of leadership theory. Plato developed this theme in his dialogues with Glaucon on the "philosopher king," as have countless religious traditions around the world. The core imperative was stated eloquently 2,700 years ago, in the Guanzi, which laid many of the foundations for Confucian social philosophy: "When a person's virtue is not equal to his position, all will suffer."

The real question for today is do we have an appetite for a renewed exploration of "doing well through doing good"? Of all the lessons I have learned from Bill O'Brien, none stands out quite so much as his resolute belief that "business success depends, over the long run, on practicing the timeless human virtues." It seems to me that in the complex world of mounting social and environmental stresses—when more and more large corporations are starting to realize that their financial bottom line is too limited a concept to assure long-term survival and vitality—the timeless wisdom of a leader like Bill O'Brien could not be more timely.

Peter M. Senge
September 2008

Acknowledgement

I wish to thank Betty Sue Flowers
for her assistance in editing this book.

— *Kathleen O'Brien Pagano*

Part 1

THE SOUL OF
AN ORGANIZATION

*These ideas are not new. But they pay
vital dividends, for they release the
human potential trapped within us
by the traditional command-and-
control approach to leadership.*

I.
THE SOUL OF
AN ORGANIZATION

The crisis inside the American corporation runs deep. It shows up when office politics dilute an organization's sense of mission, or when euphemistic language masks honestly held viewpoints, or when managers adopt a game-playing veneer that stunts their authenticity. Operating matters consume daily agendas. We have meetings to attend, reports to prepare, people to see, e-mail to read, calls to return, and deadlines to meet. Often we push aside the very values that normally steer our lives and instead simply give in to the pressure to perform.

In the race for the rational, the scientific, and the measurable, we have lost sight of something more important—an ecology in which work serves people, not only as a means for earning a living, but also as a platform on which we can develop our talents and express our best selves. The soul of an organization concerns more than matters of the bottom line.

By ecology, I mean the fundamental interrelationship of humans and their environment. An enabled ecology means that people, organizational goals, and espoused values are aligned, and that the emotional and psychological aspects of an institution are congruent with the basic, deeper, and higher attributes of human nature. Cultivating this kind of ecology requires a values-based, vision-driven leadership—a careful nurturing of the corporate culture and an acute moral awareness on the part of both managers and individual workers.

These ideas are not new. Some, indeed, are very old. If they sound "soft" to you, know that in actuality they are hard work, because they run against the grain of conventional management approaches. But they pay vital dividends, for they release the human potential trapped within us by the traditional command-and-control approach to leadership.

THE PRINCIPLE-CENTERED ORGANIZATION

In a workplace shaped by a values-based, vision-driven leadership, the goals and values of the organization are in alignment with those of the people who work there. Most important, the atmosphere stimulates people to express their highest attributes—their desire to help others, their eagerness to contribute to something larger than themselves, and their courage to stand up for what's right.

Whenever there is an ocean of information about a subject without central principles around which to organize that information, we find ourselves confused and frustrated. That is why in business we organize financial information around the income statement and balance sheet, and why we make decisions about manufacturing physical materials based on engineering principles derived from the scientific method. Through training and practice, Western management has become quite adept at resolving both financial and materialistic issues. But as a whole, it has been less successful when it comes to the management of human beings.

Since it is human beings who make the decisions and perform the actions that determine a company's results, people are arguably the most important influence on a corporation's performance in the competitive marketplace and consequently on its long-term financial achievements. Therefore, we should have principles for the governance and development of people, just as we do for financial and physical matters. Shouldn't we be striving for human excellence in corporations in the same manner as we strive for engineering or marketing excellence?

During my experience as a CEO leading cultural change, I found it necessary to constantly stimulate progress in improving both the moral climate of my organization and the individual moral maturity of the people within it. When one lagged behind the other, the community began to become dysfunctional. For example, when the value merit, which stated that all decisions should be made on the basis of what works best instead of what pleases a boss, was widely internalized in a unit and a manager was observed playing politics, feelings of betrayal and accusations of hypocrisy were generated, which worked against our business imperatives. Then again, a morally underdeveloped institutional climate usually overwhelms even the most valiant efforts of individuals to practice principle-based leadership. So I found myself constantly ratcheting up both sides of the equation to keep the ecology in balance while continuing the "never-arriving" march toward greater and greater congruence between values and behavior. A "nine" in individual moral effort with a "two" in corporate moral climate was significantly less effective than a "five" in each.

Is it possible to move an organization to a higher plane where there is less of a gap between what we say and what we do? And can you cultivate an organization that liberates the individual, pursues truth, is just, acts with courage, acquires wisdom, practices virtue— and still earns a profit?

I believe the answer to each question is yes. A climate of moral excellence can provide an enduring source of inspiration for the people who are part of it. It will also lead to high-quality service to customers, thus feeding back even greater satisfaction to the company. Naturally, a finely tuned, values-based business culture still requires a sound strategy and competent staff. But if you build on strategy and competence by nurturing the relationships in your ecology, providing a structure for honest communication and feedback, and designing processes that fill people's need for a sense of purpose, then the business imperatives of profit, market share, growth, and competitive advantage will fall into place.

WHERE TO BEGIN—A SHIFT OF MIND

The antidote to the dispiriting impact of the command-and-control, authoritarian institution is to cultivate deep respect for each individual worker, recognizing that all work has dignity and understanding that managerial humility is an important virtue for long-term success. To do this requires a shift of mind.

I am generally skeptical when someone suggests a shift of mind to me. There are too many people peddling all-purpose snake oil cures for organizational illnesses. So let me be precise about what I mean by a shift of mind.

Transformational cultural achievements require the replacement of a higher value for an inferior one, such as substituting merit-based decision making in place of political decisions, or individual responsibility in place of bureaucracy, or openness in place of unjustified secrecy. This shift of mind results in a superior mental model replacing a less effective one.

VALUES AND MENTAL MODELS

What is the difference between a value and a mental model? A value is an eternal truth about human nature that an individual believes is important and right. We live up to a value because we believe it is right to do so. We expect values to be constant.

A mental model is a set of assumptions we develop about how the world or other complex systems work so that we can process information quickly and make effective decisions. We use our mental models to decide large strategies or small tactics. The test of a mental model's effectiveness is how it works. When the outcome of a decision does not satisfy us, we should reexamine our assumptions and decide if our mental model was appropriate for the issue.

For instance, an accountant takes in information and views it through a lens that measures its impact on the income statement and balance sheet. Because of his mental model, the accountant may view the data as more important than any other information about the company. Meanwhile, the sales manager takes the same information and views it through a lens that measures customer reaction and competitive advantage. Her mental model says that, no, information from this domain is more important than any income statement or balance sheet. These two people can quickly reach an impasse about what is important unless they develop a larger, integrative mental model that encompasses both of their perspectives.

While narrow, compartmentalized mental models in the heads of employees lead to fragmented behavior in a company, integrated models encourage cooperation and competitive advantage. A larger, more overarching model helps people make more effective decisions because they can see the broader implications of their actions—not only within the company but also over time. In addition, it sharpens people's sense of the organization's overall mission; as a result, they can see how their actions contribute to the whole. When we fail to examine or revise narrow mental models, our organizations become rigid. In contrast, when we insightfully analyze and refine the models, and learn to understand others' perspectives, our organizations grow agile and our individual performance improves. Enduring competitive edge is driven not by getting the right mental model but by mastering the process of constantly improving mental models.

THE CHARACTER OF MANAGEMENT

The idea that a manager can serve his employees as well as lead was proposed by the ancient Chinese sage Lao Tzu. Robert K. Greenleaf, in his excellent book *Servant Leadership* (New York: Paulist Press, 2002, p. 240), develops the subject in a modern context, saying: "We are not wanting for knowledge of how to do things better, or for material resources to work with. But we are sorely in need of strong ethical leaders to go out ahead to show the way so that moral standards and the perceptions of many will be raised, and so that they will serve better with what they have and what they know." It is an idea whose time has returned.

Building an ecology of soul presupposes a different approach to corporate management. It respects the need for good, orderly direction but combines that with a respect for individual capacities. It understands that organizations need to serve and satisfy all members of their work family. By carefully selecting and nurturing people who espouse and practice these ideas, the leader of an organization can help shift its ecology.

But before such a shift can take place, the leader must look within his own soul and determine what he wants to do with his life—and only then what he wants his company to do. To paraphrase Gandhi, transformation takes place when you become the change that you wish to see in the world.

TRANSFORMING OUR INSTITUTIONS

The central organizing principles—the decisions and actions that involve an organization's people, values, and aspirations—cannot be reduced to a formula. Nor will there ever be a package of rules, such as there is in accounting and in science, to be plugged in and applied to human relations. It is not only unwise, but also unworkable, in this age of democracy and capitalism, to try to run an organization on principles that are forced on people. A value, by definition, can be embraced only voluntarily.

Nevertheless, there are certain values for guiding human behavior that, if followed to a reasonable degree, will transform the ecology of an organization, not only creating greater happiness and personal fulfillment in the workplace but also improving productivity and financial performance.

An organization's culture, without regard to its size, can be transformed around fewer than a dozen ideas. The most powerful transforming ideas, in my experience, are four specific corporate values and four leadership principles.

Corporate Values

Localness: *Distributing power so that decisions can be made as close to the scene of the action as possible.* Localness is more than decentralization. It is a path of discovery on which people stretch their talents to become what they are capable of becoming. Localness disperses power to competent people in an orderly, disciplined way. Over the long term, wisely distributed power produces better economic results than does centralized power.

Merit: *Evaluating decisions based on their worth, not on how much they please the boss.* Merit means directing every decision and action toward the organization's goals and aspirations while being consistent with the company's other values. Its practice eradicates the office politics that demean the dignity of people engaged in work.

Openness: *Allowing the free flow of information throughout the organization.* Since nobody has all the answers, openness is the best navigational instrument for an institution or individual to use to take stock and to chart a course.

Leanness: *Being stewards of the organization's resources.* Leanness tempers the human inclination for excess comfort and expansion, so that an organization or individual maintains its health in both good and poor economic times. It embeds in the soul of the corporation the ancient virtue of thrift.

None of these four values stands alone. Merit without openness is unachievable; openness without merit is unpalatable; merit and openness without localness leave too many people with untapped potential because they underuse their talent; and using merit, openness, and localness without leanness increases the risk that the enterprise will violate economic law and fail to prosper.

If creating value-centered cultures serves constituents so well and sounds so good, why isn't everyone doing it? Because it is hard! Because you cannot hire someone else to do it! Because it has to be done one by one until you achieve a critical mass, when the herd mentality kicks in!

Leadership Principles

A values-based, vision-driven culture is possible only when both the vision and the values of a corporation are internalized. This means that the creation of the organization's vision cannot be a top-down process but must be generated from all levels. In the twenty-first century, corporate ecologies based on values and visions will generally out-perform command-and-control corporations characterized by trickle-down disbursement of power, office politics, and bureaucracy.

The moral formation of managers occurs in a series of stages: intellectual understanding, then internalization, and finally the integration of action with beliefs or convictions. Values in the mature manager are embedded in the mind, the heart, and the hands. Being a leader in a values-based, vision-driven organization requires service, learning, and love. In the final analysis, leadership is building character and advancing learning. That is why the moral formation of our managers is of critical importance.

A learning organization aligns people and profits, values and financial performance. "How to" knowledge is technical. "What to" knowledge is directed by values and, in turn, gives direction to our lives and our organizations. A learning organization invests in human capital as the surest way to build financial capital.

A practical understanding of love starts with the understanding of the significance of work to the personal growth of the individual. Work is a platform on which people mature, develop, and achieve happiness through growing their competencies as well as contributing to the Gross World Product. Therefore, as an employee, a person is first a human being and only secondarily an instrument of production. When workers sense this order in a company, they devote quality energy to achieving the organization's business goals.

Maturity. The responsibility of leaders is to know moral principles, human nature, human needs, and human values, and how best to apply this knowledge to ordinary business tasks. We do not need to micromanage each person or situation but to know that, over time, high-quality principles will drive out low-quality principles when they are advocated by leaders with integrity who live by the values they espouse. When people are free to choose between high quality and inferior ideas, they inevitably choose the former. All people deserve a chance to have this choice in their work. Maturity is a never-ending journey. We can't teach it, but we can help one another along the road. That's what the great leaders do.

II.
WORK AND HAPPINESS

The ancient Greeks felt that those who engaged in daily work were somehow a little less than full human beings. Laborers could not be citizens and therefore could not vote. Somewhere deep inside, we still feel that work is a "necessary evil." Yet, in the modern era, work has become one of the two principle vehicles through which people seek fulfillment, a sense of purpose, and satisfaction. The other, of course, is family. In fact, for most of us, work and family are the principle stages on which we express our talents, personality, and intentions in the pursuit of becoming all we are capable of being, and therefore, presumably, of achieving happiness.

There are numerous definitions of happiness ranging from the superficial (often seen on TV commercials or in advertisements) to the profound. My personal definition of happiness goes something like this: Happiness is an inner feeling of satisfaction about my life "as a whole." This good feeling comes when I use my talents to make a contribution to something larger than myself—my family, my corporation, my nation—which should, in return, treat me fairly and appreciate my contribution. This definition distinguishes happiness from pleasure and recreation, but opposes neither. In fact, pleasure and recreation enable us to relax and refuel, reenergizing us to make contributions to further happiness.

Work and happiness are mutually reinforcing. Work is an important vehicle for achieving happiness, and happiness has its roots in devoting our talents to something larger than ourselves. It follows that creating an effective environment for work is more than getting people to do jobs efficiently in exchange for pay. Instead, designing work at any level is a near-sacred responsibility that has a powerful, direct impact on the quality of life. I remember Peter Drucker commenting that while organizations routinely say that people are their greatest asset, most still believe that people need the company more than it needs them. But in truth, organizations need more than ever to attract competent people and to provide a work environment that lets employees' talents flourish. Why? Because in the transition to the Knowledge Age, it is the new source of capital formation—the knowledge workers themselves—who control the principal means of production and give companies their competitive edge. Ensuring a high quality of work life is not just a moral imperative—it has become a business imperative.

But converting work from a "necessary evil" to a wellspring of deeper satisfaction is not about lower standards of performance or diminished financial expectations or Pollyanna thinking. In the current era of continuous improvement and high competitiveness, work must respond to people's rising expectations for fulfillment and be economically productive as well. In fact, economic effectiveness will increasingly depend upon enriching the human quality of the workplace.

HUMAN CAPITAL DRIVES FINANCIAL CAPITAL

Most seasoned entrepreneurs and managers believe that, over time, it is human capital that creates financial capital, not the reverse. Yet corporations rarely devote the same care to understanding the time-tested principles of human development as they do to applying financial and scientific principles to their tangible affairs. In fact, many organizations depreciate their human capital by unconsciously imposing financial and scientific mental models on their human relations management.

Human beings are much more than numbers and machines, however, and they have far more dimensions to them besides just the rational. Applying scientific measurements to human behavior can backfire because these reductionistic perspectives stifle creativity, ingenuity, trust, perseverance, and other gifts of human nature that directly fuel business performance and personal happiness. These essential yet intangible human qualities can flourish only if the organization itself adopts human values and lives up to them as it goes about its day-to-day business.

This notably different and more balanced approach to human relations in organizations was described by Konosuke Matsushita, the founder of the Japanese company Matsushita Electric. He once said to an English-speaking audience:

> For you, management is the art of smoothly transferring the executives' ideas to the workers' hands. For us, management is the entire work force's intellectual commitment to the service of the company […] without self-imposed functional or class barriers. Only the intellects of all employees can permit a company to live with the ups and downs and the requirements of its own new environment.[1]

What can we learn from this statement? Matsushita's message can be captured in the contrast between these two attitudes: "Tell me what you want, boss, and I'll do it," versus "Point out the direction, boss, and I'll find the best way to get there." The first attitude served corporations well during the Industrial Age, when many management higher-ups were thoroughly knowledgeable about the company and dictated procedures in order to disseminate their knowledge and run the place smoothly.

Henry Ford perhaps best embodied this idea. He knew everything about cars—from how they ran to how they should be built and maintained—and he determined how things should be done with everyone who worked for him. In those years, when businesses were seen as clocks or machines and when life in general was simpler, this kind of narrow, specific direction of employees served industries well.

As every aspect of life has grown more complex, however, the command-and-control management style has gotten increasingly difficult to maintain. Company leaders no longer know everything about the industry they work in, and the "best" or "right" way of doing things is no longer so clear. In addition, people are expecting more challenge and stimulation from their jobs than ever before. We can understand this development in the context of Maslow's hierarchy of needs. In the Industrial Era, many people worked simply to put food on the table and a roof over their heads. As our society has grown wealthier overall through industrialization, we have turned our attention from the more basic need to survive to the higher needs for acceptance and self-actualization.

Unfortunately, many senior managers fail to appreciate the impacts that the thinking, attitudes, and actions of employees at every level can have on profits, growth, efficiency, and company relation-

FIGURE 1. MASLOW'S HIERARCHY OF NEEDS

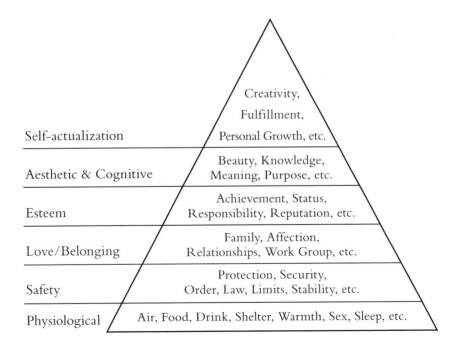

Self-actualization	Creativity, Fulfillment, Personal Growth, etc.
Aesthetic & Cognitive	Beauty, Knowledge, Meaning, Purpose, etc.
Esteem	Achievement, Status, Responsibility, Reputation, etc.
Love/Belonging	Family, Affection, Relationships, Work Group, etc.
Safety	Protection, Security, Order, Law, Limits, Stability, etc.
Physiological	Air, Food, Drink, Shelter, Warmth, Sex, Sleep, etc.

ships. In their totality, these impacts have the power either to add to or to detract from overall company performance. For example, a customer who has a notably pleasant or unpleasant experience in purchasing something by telephone from a mail-order company remembers the quality of that experience for a long time. A single interaction can influence whether that customer ever does business again with that company, or whether he or she refers others to the company. Time and attention devoted to conveying respect for all work and all employees, and for enhancing the quality of employees' thinking and the extent of their understanding of the company, can have a major impact on the organization's overall performance.

THE HIGH COST OF COMMAND-AND-CONTROL

So why haven't more companies caught on to the connection between human fulfillment at work and the financial performance of organizations? To answer this question, let's take a deeper look at the current intellectual and emotional ecology of most American businesses. Despite the trend toward "flatter" organizations, most large enterprises still in fact support outmoded bureaucracies with a top-down, command-and-control structure where people learn to play it safe. This kind of structure has numerous flaws that hamper the interpretation of information, distort decisions, and, over time, stunt the personality and character of managers and workers alike.

As a result, the corporate environment in most American institutions is drenched in personal politics that put individual interest and power-playing ahead of the enterprise's common good. In this kind of environment, "who" becomes more important than "what." Bureaucracy is used to escape personal responsibility, and complying with rules and procedures is more valued than achieving the company's intended purpose. Individuals hoard power to keep themselves up while holding others down, and aligning yourself with the right person is more important than the rightness of a decision. Finally, the pecking order reigns. People manipulate information through selective secrecy and spin control, and the company suffers an enormous waste of human and material assets in the form of "burn-out," inefficiency, and lost profits.

This unhappy scenario is not an indictment of individuals but of a system where "turf wars" and the desire for power, respect, and job security outweigh enlightened ideas about human relations. In this kind of leadership system, conformity is prized over individual commitment and involvement. This system seldom works well, even in organizations that seem to have established a modicum of order. To be sure, command-and-control gets the trains running on time, but it also takes a huge toll. It creates a climate rife with office politics, kowtowing to higher-ups, bureaucracy, and verbal gamesmanship, where human contributions such as intuition, the pursuit of truth, and the willingness to help others are devalued.

What prompts these unproductive attitudes and behaviors? The common answer is fear of job loss. We do whatever it takes to stay on the good side of whoever controls our livelihood. But there is also another, more subtle, argument at work: fear of embarrassment and of loss of respect and acceptance by one's peers. Going back to the idea of Maslow's hierarchy, nowadays many of us no longer have to worry about our actual physical survival. Instead, we have turned our attention to the higher, less-tangible levels of needs—the social levels. Unfortunately, fear of any kind is the most debilitating impediment to both learning and moral development because it blocks creativity, ingenuity, and the ability to take risks, and it dampens spirit and commitment—all essential qualities in any healthy, growing organization.

For example, in the 1970s, the quality of American cars had reached an all-time low. The cars rusted easily, were unreliable, and required expensive and frequent maintenance. As a result, imports began taking over the U.S. automobile market. But because the people on the front line in the industry felt too afraid to speak up about the problems, even though they knew of them, the American auto industry suffered a staggering blow. If those leaders at the front line had been operating within an open, merit-based corporate culture, they might well have been able to help the industry avert the difficulties that followed. Lean manufacturing combined with quality could have been invented in America instead of in Japan.

VALUES-CENTERED GOVERNANCE

If we believe that human capital drives financial capital, and not vice versa, then a values-centered organizational culture cannot be imposed. It must be inspired and voluntarily embraced.

First we must identify, understand, and internalize a set of ideas about how we govern ourselves, how we relate to one another, and what level of aspirations and standards we embrace, so that we share basic values and have reasonably common visions. This process entails forming a new, distinct culture centered on:

- ✦ deep respect for every individual, regardless of position;
- ✦ wide disbursement of power;
- ✦ high personal responsibility;
- ✦ self-discipline rather than imposed discipline; and
- ✦ a fire in everyone's belly for the organization to succeed for both consumers and investors.

Inspiring such a culture, though not easy, is the comparatively easy part. The hard part, as always, is living up to our own expectations—that is, practicing what we preach.

FIVE IDEAS ABOUT PEOPLE

We know people are complex and unpredictable. On occasion, they're funny. But their most important quality is their uniqueness. No two people are identical in appearance or personality. If people are so different, it is presumptuous to think that we can summarize them in five ideas—or even five hundred. But it is helpful in transforming a culture to have a beginning point of ideas, based on experience, from which to build.

1. There is in every person a relentless desire for happiness.

Thousands of years ago, our ancestors were hunters, leading a nomadic way of life. Every morning they had to catch the food they needed for that day. Perhaps some ten thousand years ago, the agricultural revolution began. This gave the human race the ability to store food. More than that, it allowed the development of permanent shelters and communities. But as recently as our grandparents' generation, most people had to spend nearly all of their sixty- or seventy-hour workweek earning food and shelter.

Today we no longer have to devote every minute of our working lives to earning the necessities for survival. We are able to use a much larger portion of our earnings in ways that enrich our lives. This is progress. And the engine that has driven that progress over the centuries is the relentless desire for happiness.

But if everyone possesses this desire for happiness, why isn't everybody happy? Why don't we see happiness, serenity, contentment, and peace reflected in the faces of everyone we meet? Why aren't newspapers filled with stories of a happiness quotient far exceeding that of any previous generation? And why aren't we—with all our technological progress and material goods—substantially happier than our grandparents?

At least part of the answer can be found in the words of the philosopher Mortimer Adler, who says "Happiness begins with wanting the right thing." Whether we think about it consciously or not, all of us have a mental model or image of what happiness is. These models are based on what we believe will bring us happiness. Although in real life our own models are often composites, I believe that it is useful to examine three mental models of happiness we find in society today.

1) **The Possessions/Comfort Model**

   In this model, life is viewed as a box. The object of life is to fill that box with material possessions, comfort, and pleasure.

2) **The Achievement Model**

   This model also presents life as a box to be filled, but here the object of life is to amass security, respect, power, and prestige.

3) **The Journey to Fulfill Potential**

   This third model views life not as a box to be filled but as a process, a journey toward fulfillment. The object of this journey is to become all we are capable of becoming.

Our own mental models of happiness are often more complex and seldom as clear-cut as these models. However, the model of life as a journey to fulfill our potential can do more than either of the other two models to bring us deep and lasting happiness. Embarking on this journey can also spare us that greatest of all tragedies—the realization, as we come to the end of our lives, that we have not become all we were capable of becoming.

I would like to make it very clear that I am not opposed to pleasure, comfort, or material success. On the contrary, these are actually good things. In fact, I spent most of my life in a business designed to insure people against the loss of material things through disaster or as a result of liability. But filling the boxes of material goods and security offers nowhere near the potential for happiness as seeing life as a journey to fulfill potential. And, ironically enough, those who commit to the journey to fulfill potential often find that along the way they obtain many of the tangible rewards which so often elude those who make such things their primary goal.

The model of life as a journey is built on two assumptions. The first is that each of us is a unique bundle of potential and talent. The second is that each of us has a special calling that gives direction to our journey. By "calling" I do not refer to glamorous or highly visible occupations such as entertainer, sports star, or politician. I simply mean living our lives to the fullest—whether as spouse, parent, businessperson, teacher, or police officer—so as to make a contribution to that part of society in which we find ourselves.

How do we establish a direction for our life's journey? First of all, we must decide on a destination—or at least on a direction. Would anyone set out on a vacation by walking up to an airline ticket counter and buying a ticket to "anywhere"? Yet many people set out on life's journey with scarcely more thought. This is especially unfortunate since no journey deserves more planning or pays greater dividends than does our journey through life.

As individuals, we go through three stages in deciding where we want to go on our life's journey:

✦ The first stage is the development of our personal ideas on what is important—our ideas about ourselves, our families, our relationships, our work, how society works, and how it should work.

✦ From these ideas we have to decide which are the most fundamental to us as persons and then internalize them. In other words, we must make our most deeply held beliefs part of the central core of our being.

✦ And finally, we have to bring our actions into alignment with these internalized beliefs. If our beliefs point one way, our feelings another, and our actions take us in still another direction, then we will be ripped apart inside, regardless of our status, material possessions, or physical well-being. Conversely, the alignment of our beliefs, feelings, and actions is a precondition for serenity, contentment, and happiness.

2. Work is an essential element of human happiness.

Our jobs in the world ought to be important vehicles for us in this journey to fulfill our potential. Put differently, our work should be a stage on which we strive to become all we are capable of becoming. Thus, our workplace must have a great respect for our personal alignment—that is, the correlation between what we believe and what we do.

Does this mean that our employers can never ask us to do things we don't want to do? Obviously, the answer is no. Even in an environment that emphasizes merit and openness, we can find ourselves faced with drudgery. At times we will have to disregard our preferences to achieve an important goal. But what companies have no right to ask of us is to violate those principles that are essential to our personal alignment. Moreover, companies should create an environment that assists us in our quest to fulfill our potential.

Imagine this: What would happen if every person in a company made the commitment to undertake the journey to fulfill his or her personal potential? And what if that company, in turn, supported that journey with an environment that helped each person to fulfill that potential? Imagine what that would do for each employee in the quest to fulfill his or her potential. Imagine the momentum it would give that company in its striving for unquestioned superiority.

Thirty years ago, in *The Human Side of Enterprise*, Douglas McGregor unveiled his now-famous Theories X and Y. Theory Y—with its stress on human growth and potential—began a management revolution. Before that, most corporate energy was devoted to organizing work on the basis of efficiency. Little consideration was given to the effects of work on the human beings who performed it, even though most people desire challenge and responsibility and find it natural to pursue excellence in their work.

We tend to put work into neat categories such as "blue collar" and "white collar." Federal law, for example, mandates distinctions between "exempt" and "nonexempt" workers. In manufacturing, there are often sharp distinctions between management and labor. The inference seems to be that some work is superior to other work.

But all work is ennobling. All work has dignity. What counts is not what we do but how well we do it. Martin Luther King said, "If a man is called to be a street sweeper, he should sweep streets as Michelangelo painted, as Beethoven composed music, or as Shakespeare wrote poetry. He should sweep streets so well that all the hosts of heaven and earth will pause and say, 'Here lived a great street sweeper. He did his job well.' "[2] And Vince Lombardi, the great coach of the Green Bay Packers during their dynasty in the National Football League, said, "The quality of a person's life is in direct proportion to their commitment to excellence, regardless of their chosen field of endeavor."[3] Our goal should be to use our jobs—whatever they are—to help us fulfill our potential. We do this every time we deepen our knowledge or develop our thinking, communication, or interpersonal skills.

3. The learning that drives human growth is a lifelong process.

As human beings, we all have several dimensions to our lives. We have a physical dimension that is highly dependent on nutrition. We have an intellectual dimension that is nourished by learning. And we have an emotional dimension that grows as we mature.

I don't know of anyone who stops eating when he or she graduates from school, but I am constantly amazed at the number of people who feel no need to keep learning once they complete their formal education. I consider that a tragedy.

Why do we stop learning, taking risks, and maturing? As with all complex questions, there is no simple answer. A major reason is our fear of failure. However, if we want to keep learning, we have got to risk failure. No real learning occurs without some stumbling, fumbling, and failing.

Just watch a baby learning to walk. In the process of learning to take those first half dozen independent steps, a baby falls down dozens of times. But after every fall, he or she gets up and tries again. In a matter of a few weeks, and after literally dozens of falls, the baby is able to walk across the room.

Children learn at a truly phenomenal rate, at least until the fear of failure is unintentionally programmed into them. Once we allow fear of failure to reduce our willingness to take risks, we have dramatically slowed the learning process.

Crisis often forces us to make changes that involve risk. When people are fired, suffer the loss of a spouse, or are faced with war or some other calamity, they often reach deep within themselves and draw on previously untapped resources. How wonderful it would be if we could commit ourselves to learning and taking risks—in other words, to personal growth—without requiring crisis as a catalyst.

In addition to fear of failure, another reason we stop learning is that we become victims of mental automation. By this I mean that we so mechanize routine tasks that we no longer give conscious consideration to the details, techniques, and basic assumptions.

If you don't believe you are affected by mental automation, just try to explain to a child how to tie a necktie or shoelaces. Part way into the explanation, there is a good chance you'll suddenly draw a blank on the next step. That's because your mind is no longer accustomed to dealing with the process on a conscious level.

Mental automation is essential for the daily routines of our lives. Without it, the process of doing something as simple as getting dressed would be so cumbersome that we would never be able to leave our homes in the morning. However, in a changing world, there can be severe consequences for not continuing to test the assumptions behind our mental models.

We need to constantly refine and improve our mental models in order to grow. Without that process, our mental models will remain the visions of children. Many ten-year-olds would define happiness as having plenty of junk food, the most "in" toys, and the "right" sneakers. By their late teens and early twenties, young people tend to desire respect and prestige as well as material goods. Not until they reach a certain level of experience and maturity can people choose a model of life as a journey to fulfill their potential.

4. We do not fulfill our potential in isolation but in conjunction with others.

Nature bears constant testimony to the importance of environment. In a good environment, many species of plants and wildlife will flourish. However, in a polluted environment, these same species will atrophy and perhaps even die.

So, too, with people. We perform better in an atmosphere that emphasizes trust than in one built on distrust. We are more productive in an atmosphere that encourages and empowers than in one that puts down and criticizes. We grow better in an environment that promotes freedom and independence than in one marked by regimentation and oppression.

The environment in our companies is the sum total of the ideas, attitudes, mental models, and actions of the individuals within it. A CEO doesn't have a switch in the office that controls the environment throughout the organization. That environment depends on the efforts of each of us. Since environment can have so great an impact on our growth and development, it is worth a great deal of effort to keep it positive and enriching rather than negative and restricting.

Environments tend to change almost imperceptibly. A familiar illustration of that idea is to be found in the story of the boiled frog: A frog dropped into a pot of boiling water will jump right out, instinctively recoiling from the pain. But a frog placed in a pot of cold water under which the heat is slowly turned up will be unaware of the gradual warming of the water. By the time it becomes aware of the danger, its muscles have atrophied—and it is too late to jump out.

Three aspects of the environment have a critical role in creating a values-based, vision-driven culture.

1) **Mentoring**

The eye cannot see itself. It can see other objects, but without a mirror, it cannot see itself. As human beings, we share the same limitations. We often see other people and situations quite accurately but find it hard to have real knowledge of ourselves. This is one of the reasons why it is so helpful to have a friend, mentor, or manager who cares enough to give us advice and counsel when we get off course on the journey to fulfill our potential. By tapping the ideas and insights of others—and by sharing our own—we will build the kind of environment we want.

2) **Stress**

Stress is an absorbing topic in today's society, which characterizes it as something to avoid. Yet not all stress is bad. Think for a moment of the teachers who made the greatest contribution to what you are today. Chances are they were the ones who put you under a certain amount of constructive stress.

Practically all breakthroughs are accompanied by frustration and stress. When stress leads to action and commitment in the things we can control and influence, it is constructive. When it leads to worry about things we cannot control, stress is destructive. A constructive level of stress in our organization will bring out the best in each of us and assist us in our journey for growth and development.

3) **Economic Law**

Every organization has to obey the fundamental economic law. This is true for families, communities, branch offices, hospitals, churches, insurance companies, or any entity in society—there are no exceptions. While economic theory is complex, the most fundamental economic principle is very simple: Income must exceed outgo.

Obeying that law leads to economic success, which produces the resources for an environment supportive of our quest for personal fulfillment. Simultaneously, it also provides our investors with a just return for risking their capital.

Income must exceed outgo. If we can be guided by this fundamental economic law, we will have a major advantage over those who feel that the primary purpose of economics is to attempt to predict an unpredictable future.

5. A superior level of happiness can be achieved only in conjunction with the pursuit of quality.

An organization will not distinguish itself if it tolerates mediocrity. The pursuit of quality is necessary not only for our personal growth but also for our happiness. I believe that each person possesses an inherent appetite for quality. Much of the carelessness in the business world is the result of counterproductive structures and pressures in organizations, rather than the indifference of the people who make them up.

Industry today tends to worship at the altar of three false gods which are actually the antithesis of quality in organizations. These false gods are:

1) **Growth**

Today there is an obsession with size. The goal of many companies seems to be to get bigger and bigger. Growth-driven organizations often lower their standards and engage in unsound economic expansion. Growth should be a natural outcome of our commitment to quality. We should grow because our reputation for quality is so high that more and more people seek to do business with us. Even then, we cannot allow ourselves to grow beyond our ability to deliver quality. If necessary, we must limit growth to maintain quality. Yet large numbers of companies allow the appetite for growth to outpace the appetite for quality. The result, inevitably, is trouble.

2) **Greed**

This is an extension of the desire for growth. The business press is full of examples. There is, for instance, the on-going contest between the major players in the soft drink market who are pulling out all the stops for a fraction of a point of market share. People's Express provides another example. This airline reached a billion dollars in sales faster than any other start-up corporation in America, and it opened air travel to many people who had not been able to afford it. It was widely hailed as one of the outstanding companies of its time. And then it got caught up in a desire to be everything—and fast. Its purchase of Frontier, a company which stood for few of the things that had propelled People's Express to success, led to severe financial and service problems. The almost predictable result of this overrapid expansion was the loss of its own identity.

3) **Goodies**

Big, successful institutions tend to lose sight of their original mission of serving the customer. They begin to put the emphasis on serving themselves, increasing their comfort levels, their benefits. Those who made them successful—the customers—are all but forgotten. This is often evident in executive circles. Executives of large companies may have private airplanes and limousines; they select the biggest room in the best hotel; and they begin to lose sight of the purpose of the business. They come to equate quality with buying the best.

Anyone can buy quality, particularly when he or she is spending someone else's money. The kind of quality we should be concerned about is the quality we produce. That is the kind of quality that can help both individuals and organizations reach their potential. That is the kind of quality Martin Luther King and Vince Lombardi invited us to strive for.

THE PRINCIPLE OF SYNERGY

The achievement of our personal potential is one of life's most exciting and rewarding experiences. As all of us improve as individuals, the organization improves; and as the organization improves, the opportunities increase for each of us within it.

A question can legitimately be raised about this thesis. Is it possible to harmonize the goals of both the individual and the organization? Or is this unity a myth perpetuated by management to obtain greater productivity from its members?

Much of the progress in Western civilization over the last three hundred years has come from separating and specializing. Splitting the atom has led to scientific progress; splitting the cell has opened up medical horizons. Though there are strong interconnections among medicine, psychology, theology, economics, and philosophy, we tend to treat each field of knowledge as separate and distinct, dividing each area into specialties and even subspecialties. However, without an understanding of the interrelatedness of things, it is only a short jump from specialization to polarization. Thus we have situations in which integral parts of the whole often act in opposition to each other: capital versus labor, the organization versus the individual, conservationists versus industrialists. In many ways we have become an us-versus-them society.

All too often overlooked is the power of working together. The word synergy, a medical term used by the early Greeks, comes from an understanding of this power. Syn means together and ergo means to work. The human body is a good example of synergy in action. Reduced to its chemical components, the body of the most brilliant scientist or philosopher is worth less than $10. Yet who can put a price tag on the value of the living scientist or philosopher? What good is an eye without a mind to interpret and understand? Of what use is a hand without the brain to direct it? The beauty, productivity, and value of the human body come from its unity—the synergy of all the parts, working together.

The world of sports provides other examples of this power. There are teams made up of highly talented players, but which never seem to achieve much. And there are teams in which the accomplishments of the team far transcend the individual talents of the players. What accounts for the latter? Though there are many and complex reasons, an important one is the ability of rather ordinary players to become an extraordinary team by unleashing the power of synergy.

Every employee who embarks on a journey to fulfill his or her personal potential will make a significant contribution to the organization as a whole and to the organization's quest for superior performance. In addition, embarking on this journey to fulfill potential is the surest route to genuine personal happiness. If we do not set limits to our own personal growth and the growth of others, there are no limits to the synergistic forces we can place in motion.

1. Konosuke Matsushita, *Not By Bread Alone* (New York: Berkley Books, 1994).
2. Martin Luther King Jr. used this example in several speeches, including in "The Birth of a New Age" on August 11, 1956, in Chicago.
3. Vince Lombardi, *Second Effort* (video).

Part 2

CORPORATE VALUES

Good values are antidotes to inferior behavior. We live up to our values, even when it is difficult, because we believe it is right to do so.

III.
LOCALNESS

I n this time of accelerating change, many of us believe we have less and less influence on events. Disillusionment with large institutions—government, business, education—has prompted many of us to lower our personal and professional aspirations and conclude that we have no say in how things are run. Though no one likes mediocrity, we tend to tolerate it. In nearly all companies, people have come to learn to accept the world this way, and a kind of "play it as it lays" fatalism prevails.

But what if we believed we could change our part of the world? What if organizations valued our opinions and let us know that our decisions would make a difference? What would such a company look like? What values would it espouse?

THE POWER OF THE LOCAL

Most managers agree that the best decisions are made as close to the scene of action as possible because people become highly motivated when they feel accountable for their own actions and results. This is the essence of the idea of localness: Making decisions as close to the scene of action as is practical. When people are given this kind of decision-making responsibility, they develop a sharp sense of the possible unintended consequences of their decisions. They also learn to trust the wisdom of their intuition. Armed with an awareness of the context within which their decision will play out, they can weigh important nuances and "shades of gray" that have a bearing on the decision. Localness thus helps people to make the best decisions possible.

WHAT LOCALNESS ISN'T

+ First of all, localness is not a geographic distinction. It is not simply a management approach, like decentralization, that places operating functions and certain authority outside headquarters.

+ Localness is not a way for local managers or branches to gain control at the expense of the CEO or national office. It does not imply that an individual or branch can feel "It's my decision and I'll do whatever I want" or "I don't have to be responsible to anyone" or "Since I know more than anyone else about what has to be done, I don't have to explain."

+ Localness is not unlimited authority. Authority based on power destroys merit. The concept of merit is essential to localness; authority based on power is antithetical to localness.

+ Localness cannot be demanded or imposed by others. Neither can it be thrust downward in an organization.

+ Localness is not limited to branches or departments or units located outside the national office. It also applies to relationships among functions within a company.

WHAT LOCALNESS IS

At the basic level, localness is an organizational design that lets each person use his or her job both to develop personally and to serve the organization's mission. It comprises a set of attitudes, ideas, and actions that lead to effective decisions, that guide relationships between people at various levels in the company, and that maintain a balance between order and freedom. Localness is actually harder to practice than command-and-control, for it is much more complicated to be free than to be enslaved.

✦ Localness combines a high level of personal responsibility and confidence in oneself with the understanding that key decisions should be tested by discussion with those who can add specialized knowledge, experience, or objectivity. Localness demands a mature willingness to use all the resources available. It is the only way we can combine the advantages of both local and national or global companies while avoiding the disadvantages of each.

✦ Localness is not so much a division of authority as it is a division of functions. Localness says that those functions that can be accomplished more effectively at the local level should be; those that can be carried out more effectively at the national level should be.

✦ Localness is also a matter of emphasis. In most companies, important decision making is reserved for the home office unless there is a demonstrable reason for it to be in the branches. Localness transforms this relationship, however, positioning decision making in the local branches unless there is a demonstrable reason to have it in the headquarters office.

✦ Localness says that people who live, work, and socialize at the local level should be able to determine the needs of the local market and local agents more effectively than people in the national office. But local people, who are close to the action, are absorbed in meeting local needs, and are working under strong local pressures, rarely can have the perspective that national people can have. When a broad perspective and technical resources are integrated with local knowledge, experience, and ability, the result will be superior performance.

✦ Localness requires national people to stretch their abilities to meet the needs of local staffs. Through carefully selected strategies and training, they can also help branches accomplish in a few years what might take twice as long using trial-and-error methods.

✦ Localness is a philosophy that guides people who are at different levels of an organization in relating to one another. National offices help local branches find ways to accomplish their goals. Local managers get feedback—reinforcement for things that go well and assistance in changing those things that don't work.

✦ Localness requires the liberation of workers at all levels from the oppressive features of the command-and-control structure, so that each individual may use the job to develop personally and to serve the organization's mission. Rather than simply capitulating to order, localness embraces the tension between order and freedom.

✦ Localness is a spirit, a way of life that grows out of personal conviction and that is made possible by the acceptance of individual responsibility and self-direction.

✦ Localness is crucial to the concept that work can serve as a primary vehicle through which people achieve satisfaction and happiness—that it can engage the whole person.

Here's an insurance industry example of localness in practice: Imagine two underwriters, each at a different company. Both underwriters receive a particularly difficult insurance proposal that has some mitigating circumstances, and each must decide whether to accept or reject the proposal. Underwriter A works at a company that ignores the value of localness. This underwriter simply processes the application using the standard formulas for assessing risk. Underwriter B, whose company practices a large degree of localness, takes it upon herself to do a little research before deciding her next step. She meets with the agent who developed the proposal and gets more information about the mitigating circumstances behind the situation. She also decides to gather a group of agents to discuss the challenges facing underwriters dealing with this particular kind of insurance hazard.

In taking this initiative, underwriter B develops skills in researching, organizing, and running meetings, and perhaps even public speaking if she facilitates the meeting. She becomes much more than someone who just follows orders and fills out forms. Her actions lead to an even more valuable benefit: they encourage the exchange of ideas and strengthen the professional community in which she works.

So how do we go about designing jobs that are both liberating and economically productive?

THE PRINCIPLE OF SUBSIDIARITY

Surprisingly, localness is not simply a modern idea. Its roots stretch back to the medieval principle of subsidiarity, which centered on the concept of freedom from the oppression of feudal society. The principle of subsidiarity states that it is a usurpation of good order for a higher, more powerful level of people (for example, nobles) to intervene at a lower level (for example, merchants), especially if the people at the lower level are capable of resolving the issues themselves. The application of this principle is as appropriate to twenty-first-century business enterprise as it was to twelfth-century feudal fiefdoms. It applies across the full spectrum of human relations in organized settings, whether the situation involves the headquarters of a multinational corporation and a remote field office, or a cook and a dishwasher in a small eatery.

Under the principle of subsidiarity, the role of the national office is to serve as the center or core of an organization. As such, it has the responsibility of developing its central philosophies, establishing its strategic direction, and uplifting the aspirations that govern its standards. This role requires deep thought, specific business knowledge, sound judgment, effective communication, and the kind of enlarged integrity that encourages wide followership.

The national staff should function as a resource as well as a detached viewpoint, helping branch personnel make effective decisions. By developing programs and services that are needed by many branch offices, the national office eliminates duplication and promotes efficiency; it also makes such programs and services available to branches still in the process of developing their own resources. And finally, the national staff provides the financial reports and scorecards that measure operating performance.

But of all its responsibilities, none is more important than that of promoting a desire for personal growth, which helps its people become stronger and more effective.

Job Design—The Local Is the Personal

If we believe that each person has the ability to grow, and that one of our most important responsibilities is to help ourselves and others grow, then first we must create an environment that will encourage personal growth—that will, in fact, make us uncomfortable if we don't grow. But growth, whether personal or corporate, will happen only if we value it enough to work for it.

Second, we must overcome the traditional pattern of focusing job training on technique alone. To fully engage a person, work must be understood in its context—how it fits into the larger function of the company or competitive universe. But it must also be understood in its aspirational dimension—what we would like to achieve in the future.

Most people entering an organization that promotes localness have received their professional training in command-and-control companies. A few might think that since there is less of the apparatus and baggage they were accustomed to in their command-and-control days, they now can do anything they want to do. That, of course, is false. Localness does not mean an absence of discipline. In an organization that promotes localness, the discipline springs from common values and shared aspirations, and often takes the form of a sense of personal accountability. Discipline therefore means self-discipline, not externally imposed discipline. Internalizing accountability can be a tough transition for those who have not been encouraged to develop personal responsibility or to express their creative selves—but once accomplished, it is a source of joy.

LOCALNESS AND POWER

Localness does not alter the source of authority in an organization. In all public corporations, for example, decision-making power flows from shareholders to an elected board of directors to the CEO, and on through echelons of management, just as it does under the conventional hierarchical arrangement. What does change under the philosophy of localness is how managers choose to use and distribute their power. Over time, distributing power to capable people increases organizational adaptability and self-reliance. Conversely, hoarding power at each echelon increases rigidity and decreases individual responsibility at the critical points where the rubber meets the road. Organizations that widely distribute power to competent people will generally out-perform those with equally competent people who tend to hoard power at each echelon.

Power is also one of those rare commodities that, if given away with care and discrimination, actually increases. The more power you give away, the more influence you retain. This may sound like a paradox, but think about that for a moment. When you disperse power, you do not give up responsibility or influence—that would be abdication. Instead, localness entails giving workers or subordinate levels of managers the authority to make decisions and own the results of those decisions, the understanding of the context surrounding issues they are likely to face, and a familiarity with the company's larger aspirations. In my experience, managers who delegate power effectively produce a better economic performance than those who do not. As a result, their superiors end up asking them to take on more responsibility—and thus they acquire more power and influence.

Cultivating localness starts with asking a fundamental question: "What is the best way to use and distribute power?" rather than "Who gets the power?" The word empowerment is important here. Unfortunately, however, it has been only partially understood. The misuse of the term has even led to the assumption that dispersing power means giving up order and discipline. Empowering employees means encouraging them to develop their best professional selves while still maintaining order in the company.

Distributing power strengthens self-discipline and helps an organization achieve an optimum mix of both imposed rules and personal accountability. By nurturing the self-discipline side of this equation, managers encourage flexibility and a "can-do" spirit on the part of employees. Generally, a company with high self-discipline has a competitive advantage over one that relies heavily on enforced discipline. Why? Self-discipline engenders flexibility and spirit. "Let's figure out what to do and the best way to do it" is a more productive mind-set than "Tell me what you want, boss, and I'll do it." Employees who feel that their role is limited to following orders only grow more dependent on supervision. Their managers, in turn, become trapped in the role of volunteer fireman, always having to react to emergencies and grapple with the details themselves. Self-discipline, by contrast, frees managers to spend more of their time on the larger issues of designing strategy and nurturing a productive culture.

You may be thinking "But what manager is going to want to give up power?" After all, many business leaders believe that their power hinges on their ability to "stay on top of things," which often looks to employees like "micromanagement." But imagine a different scenario: replacing micromanaging with high expectations. Expectations have far more power than micromanaging does to influence behavior—especially when both managers and employees aspire to those expectations. In fact, repeated studies have shown that one of the most effective ways to influence someone else's behavior is to clearly and precisely convey what you expect of him or her.

Equally important, internally generated motivation builds capacities such as creativity, ingenuity, and relationship-building skills—all of which spring from self-motivation. In an age when the quality of physical products is fairly even across industries, these intangible qualities have now become the distinguishing features in many industries' products and services.

But here's the most compelling reason to build a corporation's culture on widely dispersed power and high personal responsibility: These values encourage employees to mature into their most complete selves. As people mature personally, they achieve a healthy balance between focus on self and focus on others. Thus they become more able and eager to take responsibility for helping others and to contribute to "something larger." Mature individuals also find it easier to resolve conflicts; they can see things from others' perspective, and their ability to focus on what is best for the company overall prevents them from getting entangled in petty rivalries or narrow problems. Consequently, problems get resolved before they blow up into disruptive, expensive disasters.

Finally, maturity at work has a crucial ripple effect at home: as we mature, we become better citizens, spouses, and parents. We can take what we have learned about collective responsibility at the workplace and apply it to our family and community life. Conversely, if our immaturity prevents us from getting the ultimate fulfillment from our work, our dissatisfaction becomes apparent to others. This can be especially harmful in families. When parents come home grumbling about their day at the plant or the office, their children also grow up thinking of work as "a necessary evil."

After all this discussion about localness, you may be wondering whether giving front-line people the opportunity to reach their full potential negates the need for senior managers. In fact, these leaders retain a distinct role—helping people grow through mentoring, coaching, evaluating, inspiring, clarifying principles, and articulating overarching values and the organization's mission. From their unique perch at the core of the organization, senior executives have serious responsibilities for setting the organization's long-term direction.

LOCALNESS AND VALUES

The degree of localness is determined as we apply our values to specific situations through discussion with the people involved. Competent people who have a vision of what they want to become, who share common values, and who believe in decision making based on merit will usually come up with the best answer. In those instances in which we cannot reach agreement, we must fall back on the authority inherent in an organization's structure. However, such instances should be exceedingly rare if we are committed to our values and if we practice them reasonably well.

LOCALNESS DOESN'T MEAN YOU'RE ALONE

There are few things we can't accomplish if we want to enough. Sometimes, however, there is a difference between what we think or say we want and what we actually want. This happens not because we are dishonest but because we are not fully aware of all the factors.

Managers, for instance, may feel they want to run their own shows. Lurking in the backs of their minds, however, may be a fear that if they have the responsibility, they will have no place to hide when mistakes occur. That's natural. But localness doesn't mean you're out there all alone. It simply means that some people have the responsibility and accountability—and they can call on national staff members for counseling and support when they need it. An analogy for this design can be seen in the relationship between the family and the state. The local office is a natural family group. Small is beautiful, and families can achieve things that cities or states could never accomplish. But families do not have all the resources they need. Hence, the necessity for the city and state.

MANAGING LEVELS IN AN OPEN ORGANIZATION

Levels are natural and necessary in any group of human beings who band together to improve life by performing an economic, academic, or government service. We see this in business (home office, regional offices, and branches), in government (federal, state, county, city), and in education (superintendent, principal, faculty).

Levels have long been a source of organizational problems in American business, as well as in large insurance companies. Relations between levels frequently cause a counterproductive friction that has a negative effect on the quality and quantity of work and that causes workers to "turn off" on their jobs. But there are ways to establish relationships in which each level contributes to the growth and fulfillment of the others.

To begin with, we should not confuse the natural order of levels in an organization with any notions of inferiority or superiority of the individuals who occupy positions at the various levels. Individuals should serve at the level for which their unique talents—at a particular time in their careers—are best suited, or where current circumstances happen to place them. A great enterprise needs outstanding people both on the front lines and at the center. A person's worth to the enterprise is determined by what he or she contributes—not by where he or she is located.

Attaining optimum relationships between levels in an organization is a difficult and painstaking task—though I can think of none that is more critical to success. Of course, there are practical observations that we can make about levels—such as that the shorter the distance between the front lines and the center, the better; or that the fewer the levels, the better. But there are two fundamental assumptions that are key to managing levels in an organization: First, that in general, the participants in our mission are competent. And second, that they generally agree on the purpose and the vision of the company and share a conviction about the rightness of the company's values.

THE ASSUMPTION OF COMPETENCE: OVERCOMING THE PROTECTIONIST IMPULSE

Organizational structure and philosophies can be designed to protect a company from incompetence. Many, perhaps most, companies unconsciously have this as a primary goal. But an organization that puts strong emphasis on a design to protect itself from incompetence will eventually incur a form of paralysis from the rigidity it inflicts on people. This rigidity stifles initiative, creativity, and motivation in many individuals.

If we are afflicted with intractable incompetence, either in the field or at headquarters, we must change that situation instead of designing an operating philosophy to defend ourselves from it. To do otherwise inevitably stifles energy and limits achievement.

A SHARED CONVICTION: LEADING BY MORAL SUASION

The national staff leads best when it leads by moral suasion. What is moral suasion? It is simply the ability to help guide others to the best answer, combined with integrity at the center that convinces others that you, as well as your reasoning, can be trusted.

Obviously, localness is more than a geographic designation. It is those attitudes, ideas, and principles that lead to better decisions, guide relationships between levels, and maintain a balance between order and freedom to encourage the growth of people at all levels of an organization.

IV.
MERIT

I f localness is about liberating individuals, then the value merit is about liberating ideas. In fact, the two values are linked: Localness frees people to generate ideas about their own work, and merit encourages the judging of those ideas based on their inherent worth, not on their degree of political connivance. In a merit-based organization, people strive to attain the organization's purpose and vision in a way that is consistent with its values and strategy—that is, what it stands for and intends to achieve.

Three kinds of environments dominate the world of organizations: bureaucratic, political, and merit. Most organizations are not pure versions of one of these forms, but contain the seeds of each.

A bureaucratic environment is one in which compliance with rules and procedures is more important than accomplishing the intended purpose. In fact, most members of a bureaucratic organization seldom identify with its purpose. Those who do identify become frustrated by the red tape. In a bureaucratic environment, people soon learn to think bureaucratically. "Don't use your own judgment. Don't take risks. Don't worry about what you think is right or more effective. Play it safe. Follow the rules."

A political environment emphasizes the fulfillment of the wishes and expectations of an individual. The "who" is stressed rather than the "what." There are several disadvantages of a political environment. First, people aim to please the boss by saying what they think the boss wants to hear instead of what he or she should know—scoring points

47

becomes more important than advancing the organization's mission. Second, it is difficult to get various elements to work together for the overall good of the organization because the focus of attention is on making certain individuals look good. Third, advancement depends on aligning oneself with the right person and pleasing that person, instead of on contributing to the organization's results.

In a merit environment, the entire effort of the organization is focused on the attainment of the organization's purpose and vision in a way that is consistent with its values. It is characterized by careful evaluation of the merits of any idea, not by the attitude of "Who's in charge here" or "It's right because the boss says it's right." It is an environment where people can say, "We carefully gathered the facts, discussed them freely, and now believe we can set the most appropriate course."

A merit environment, in contrast to a bureaucratic or a political environment, supports individual initiative, open discussion, and the search for the common good.

The idea of merit is startlingly simple, logical, and sensible. Why, then, is it so often eclipsed by the politics of self-interest or bureaucracy? The reason is that creating a merit environment requires most of us to change the way we think and express our thinking. Practicing merit requires a strong sense of responsibility and a willingness to speak out—not to blindly follow commands for order's sake, but to focus on ways to achieve the organization's purpose and vision that are consistent with its values. The challenge of merit is to practice it so that behavior is consistent with what we say and what we intend.

How do we get there? How do we create and sustain the dedication required for a merit environment?

THE FOUR PILLARS OF A MERIT ENVIRONMENT

Pillar 1: Clarity of Purpose

The very meaning of merit in any situation depends on what you are trying to accomplish. It must be tied to your purpose, your vision, and your values. Employees must understand the company's purpose and goals, and the reasoning behind them. This means that senior managers must become much better at explaining the business context and challenges to those who report to them.

Pillar 2: Fact Gathering

Whenever there is a situation that someone believes should be examined to promote greater effectiveness, the first step is to assemble as many facts as feasible about the situation. This brings us squarely into conflict with a piece of common wisdom— that everyone has a right to his or her own opinion. In a merit environment, this simply isn't true. If I don't have sufficient facts to understand the situation, analyze it, and arrive at a responsible conclusion—right or wrong— then I don't have a right to an opinion in a group discussion.

For the merit environment to work effectively, each person has to share the responsibility for getting and analyzing the facts. Each person has to do his or her homework. There is no easy way, no shortcut. We have to take the responsibility of thinking about the merits of our ideas, rather than raising questions or making suggestions just because we want something changed. People who don't know what they are talking about because they haven't done their homework don't help solve problems in a merit environment. They can't even know what the merits are if they haven't gathered enough facts.

Pillar 3: Open Discussion

After doing our homework, we must sort out and test the merits of our conclusions through open, candid, free discussion. People must also feel free to question rules and procedures and to speak out whenever something stands in the way of achieving the organization's purpose. Creating a merit environment means encouraging individuals to express their thoughts about what they are doing or should be doing.

At this point you can run across two potential pitfalls. First, some people may not believe you actually want to discuss the merits. They may not even have done their homework because they believe you want a rubber stamp type of agreement, not an evaluation and discussion based on merit.

Second, once the discussion gets going and each person puts forward his or her conclusion and reasoning, there is a strong temptation to want to "win the argument" for the pure competitive satisfaction of winning, regardless of the merits. This competitive spirit can seriously affect the merit discussion process unless we understand that winning for each of us and the group means arriving at the most effective, most meritorious solution. For many of us, this is a drastic change in thinking and behavior and requires constant self-discipline.

Pillar 4: Nurturing an Ongoing Strategic Dialogue

Leaders can do a number of things to nurture an ongoing strategic dialogue. First, they can introduce the core competencies of learning, such as conversation skills and systems thinking, to their departments through workshops and other types of training. Second, they can constantly strive to understand, challenge, and enrich their own mental models. Third, they can honor reflection by allowing time for it.

I experienced the benefits of reflection firsthand at Hanover. For example, one day during our early work on purpose and values, I became so frustrated with the organization's drifting that I decided to take a day off and relax by the pool. As I lay there soaking up the sun, I kept brooding about the list of slogans and clichés we had generated while trying to ascertain our core values. I couldn't resist the temptation to map them out on a spreadsheet. As I looked them over in frustration, trying to figure out what they could mean for Hanover, the idea of values suddenly clicked into place in my mind as a useful underpinning for improvement in our culture. I introduced my ideas to my colleagues some time later, and eventually, after a long period during which these ideas "percolated" in the company, we began to internalize the values of localness, merit, openness, and leanness.

Identifying the four values was just the beginning; from there we were able to move forward in building a culture that demanded—and received—more from all of us.

Of course, sitting by the pool for a day isn't always the most practical way of allowing time for reflection. But if managers could find ways to incorporate reflection time into their daily dealings at work, and to let others know how much they value its importance, perhaps more creative ideas would emerge.

A fourth contribution leaders can make toward nurturing strategic dialogue seems simple: during meetings, they can set the agenda at a pitch so that people don't "drown in the details." Managers can also help by explaining the larger context of the department's work to those who report to them. In my own work with an oil company, I witnessed how important it is to explain context and to "decompartmentalize" knowledge—in any industry. Within this oil company was a group that focused on finding oil. Managers in this group supervised geologists who actually looked for oil deposits. These managers understood the financial ramifications of drilling for oil. For example, some oil might be so expensive to acquire that drilling in that location would not be financially worthwhile. Unfortunately, however, the managers did not share this information with the individual geologists whose job it was to look for oil deposits. As a result, the geologists invested enormous time, effort, and money in targeting all the oil deposits they could find. If they had known more about the financial ground rules of drilling in various locations, they would have been able to make wiser suggestions—without wasting so many resources.

For merit to work, people must take responsibility for thinking about the usefulness of their ideas, rather than raising questions or making suggestions just because they want to see something changed. Questions like: "Will the idea help us to accomplish our purpose more effectively?" or "What are the facts?" or "What decisions seem best after we openly discuss the facts and relate them to improving effectiveness?" all encourage a merit environment. Merit is thus characterized by careful evaluation of the worthiness of ideas. In a merit environment, people say: "We carefully gathered all the necessary facts, discussed them freely, and now believe we can set the most appropriate course."

Out of this continual testing and challenging of individual ideas and actions, new insights will emerge that will generate fresh strategies and shape goals. The organization's strategy and goals thus evolve with input that is not just top-down and bottom-up but also "bounced around." Decisions that stem from a merit environment are better informed and more widely owned by the people involved in crafting them.

HEIGHTENED ROLE FOR MANAGEMENT

When people believe that what they are doing is worth doing, and when they know they can change the way their department or the company operates, then organizations get better ideas and better results. People have more fun at work and feel a greater degree of satisfaction because their whole person is utilized—body, mind, and spirit. The role of management changes, too, from one of "boss" to one characterized by the phrase "leadership by example." While managers have the same authority and responsibility as they would have in comparable organizations, for a merit environment to work, managers must be able to teach what the vision and values are all about and to apply the vision and values to local needs. Further, institutional frameworks must support managers and help the company's governing ideas and strategic mental models to pervade the organization.

WHICH ENVIRONMENT WILL PREVAIL?

No organization exists without an environment. If a merit environment is not actively worked at, a bureaucratic or political environment will set in. We cannot maintain a merit environment if we are passive.

Nor can a merit environment be imposed from the top down. The degree to which we enjoy the advantages of a merit environment and avoid the disadvantages of the other kinds of environments depends on the commitment of each person in the organization. And this commitment stems directly from a personal conviction about the kind of people we want to be and the kind of organization we want to help build.

V.
OPENNESS

L ike localness and merit, a third value—openness—is also tightly intertwined with the other values. Openness refers to the unfettered flow of information and ideas throughout an organization. It is essential for a merit environment because it lets us gather the data we need to evaluate the worth of ideas.

The free flow of information often happens easily in our social lives—we share feelings and information with others and invite them to do the same. Yet in organizational life, openness suddenly becomes much more difficult. Have you ever attended a meeting where you disagreed with what was being said, but you did not feel free to voice your own ideas? Did you then leave the meeting at break to become involved in a discussion where people felt they could say what they really thought? If your answer is yes, you're not alone. Many people sit through such events thinking, "I don't believe that's the right thing to do" or "I'd like to say what I think, but I know my boss doesn't agree" or "I'd better keep quiet about my ideas; they're just too different." Then, they vent in the corridors or the lavatories.

An open environment attempts to resolve this tension. It seeks to create a climate in which people can share their ideas without worrying about whether others will be pleased or offended, without considering who is for or against an idea, without keeping track of "winners" and "losers." But while it is one thing to say you want to be open, it is another thing to practice it. Why is openness so difficult?

All of us were born with unlimited potential for openness, but we seem to lose the ability to exercise it as we get older. As adults, we often struggle to reclaim the spontaneity that came to us so naturally as young children. One reason for this loss is that most of us were conditioned during our formative years by experiencing more win-lose than win-win situations, more "shall nots" than "can dos," more distrust than trust, more competition than cooperation. These lessons start when we are small and get socially institutionalized in many ways. In such a world, there is every reason to play our cards close to our vest—and very little incentive to be open. So how can we build environments that encourage openness?

BUILDING OPEN ENVIRONMENTS

Openness is like a lubricant, encouraging the free flow of information and the meaningful discussion essential to sound decisions. When practiced, it lets us know what is happening, why it is happening, and what thinking lies behind decisions and actions. It results in decisions that incorporate multiple viewpoints and experiences.

We build open environments by being honest with each other; sharing our thoughts and opinions; developing mutual understanding of our company's purpose, vision, and values; sharing information; respecting ourselves and others; helping each other succeed; and "walking our talk," that is, striving for close alignment between our words and our behavior.

Openness has four dimensions—conversation skill, listening, information flow, and trust and credibility. Each dimension is connected with the others, as we usually find when we explore values in the context of developing our philosophy.

Conversation Skill

Most of us have a strong drive to accomplish our own agendas—to attend to the goals for which we feel the most intense passion. In working single-mindedly toward these goals, we strive to exert control over tasks, and to maximize our "wins" and minimize our "losses." But this narrow focus can lead us to make only token commitments to the goals of the company. It also fosters a low quality of conversation often characterized as verbal gamesmanship. Protective of our own agendas, we are guarded around others, say what we think others want to hear, and avoid raising "delicate" issues.

Picture another kind of conversation, one marked by passion, deep insights, and the freewheeling exchange of ideas. What kind of attitudes would people need to hold to create this environment? For one thing, participants at a business meeting would take the initiative in expressing their ideas and opening themselves to the responses of others. They would work under the assumption that ideas are being presented for testing, not for sale. These participants would see the sharing of information as essential to both individual and organizational growth. In addition, the capacity to inquire about the beliefs and ideas of another would be given equal weight to the ability to advocate ideas.

Some people have highly developed advocacy skills and are willing to put their ideas forward—to tell others what is on their minds. High-advocacy individuals let others know exactly where they are coming from. We don't have to be mind readers to know where they stand or what they are recommending. Low-advocacy individuals tend to hold back. They use ambiguous or guarded language that can leave others uncertain or confused. Their reluctance to take a stand makes them seem "firmly committed to the middle of the road."

Advocacy promotes openness as long as we do not express our opinions so strongly that we discourage others from expressing theirs. Supervisors and managers especially should remind themselves how intimidating it can be to differ with "the boss." Winning is arriving at the best answer, not dominating. Conversation skill requires clarity, the ability to use dialogue, and the willingness to pursue negotiation. Conversation skill also requires the habit of reflecting on one's own thinking.

Listening

The capacity of an individual to inquire about the beliefs and ideas of the other person is as important as the ability to advocate. Inquiry involves seeking the ideas of others as well as their reactions to our ideas. High-inquiry individuals communicate a genuine interest in the ideas of others, openness to other points of view, and a willingness to have their points of view challenged.

Inquiry requires a highly developed ability to listen. Listening is an active process that demands effort and concentration. It rewards the listener with new insights, and more and better information and ideas. We can build our capacity to listen by wanting to hear what others have to say. We can also become more sensitive to habits that get in the way of effective listening, such as:

+ Not listening because we are certain our own ideas are right.

+ Not paying attention because we think we already know what the other person is going to say.

+ Pretending to listen but putting very little effort into understanding.

+ Planning what we will say the moment the other person takes a breath.

+ Listening only until we disagree, then interrupting to present our point of view.

+ Being distracted, thinking of other things, not really caring to listen.

We can replace faulty listening habits with effective ones by cultivating the following attitudes:

✦ Listening actively rather than passively by seeking understanding, accuracy, and clarity.

✦ Listening for the total meaning, including what is assumed or simply unsaid.

✦ Listening with reflection—repeating the message in our own words and asking if our interpretation is accurate.

✦ Listening with an open mind—realizing that through a free and open exchange of ideas and insights, we arrive at the best solutions.

Obviously, we need to balance advocacy and inquiry. Too much advocacy with too little inquiry—speaking our minds candidly but being less willing to hear the ideas of others—puts others on the defensive and inhibits the free flow of information. On the other hand, a high level of inquiry with very low advocacy—listening to others but seldom indicating what we are thinking—comes across as indifference and robs others of our ideas and insights. By balancing advocacy and inquiry, we increase communication, reduce misunderstanding, and create the environment necessary for merit-based decisions.

Information Flow

Sharing information is essential for the capacity of both individuals and the organization to grow. In order to fully engage the whole person in work—spirit, mind, body—everyone has to know the rules of the game, how the company is performing relative to its goals and competitors, and what critical issues the company faces. Knowledge is power, so to be open is to share power. To share power, managers must confront the fear of loss of control and status, while the organization must reward not power but empowering.

There should be no hoarding of information, no pockets of secrecy, and no indiscussible subjects. Of course, exceptions to full information flow are necessary in the case of data entailing individual privacy (the content of a performance review) or insider information. However, in general, everyone has access to all fifty-two cards in the deck—and in the case of meetings, preferably several days before the date set for discussion. Preparing for a meeting in this way lets people digest the information and form opinions and insights ahead of time, and keeps people from presenting information at the last minute in order to manipulate opinion. In addition, the scorecard on which people are judged must be fair and visible to everyone.

Trust and Credibility

It is impossible to have openness without trust. Through trust we accept the risks that come with open and honest communication because we care about others, the organization, and ourselves. Without trust, people feel isolated. They experience a drop in their confidence and self-esteem, and they tend to choose security over risk. The result is often a decline in both individual happiness and organizational effectiveness. Trust is based on a mutual confidence in the character, competence, strength, truthfulness, and caring of another. There is no easy route to a trusting relationship: both parties must earn it by being trustworthy. And the first step toward trustworthiness is credibility.

Many people think business leaders are smart. Far fewer people think they are believable. This is because there are often huge gaps between official business statements and reality. Out-and-out lying is probably infrequent, but slanting or putting "spin" on information to manipulate readers or listeners or to protect one's position is, unfortunately, quite common. American corporate managers have become so accustomed to putting a spin on information that many are no longer conscious of doing it. Bad financial news is obscured by relegating it to a footnote on page 32 of the annual report. New words like "rightsizing" are coined to describe layoffs that result from unwise past decisions. You often get the feeling of drowning in molasses when companies report news in their house organs, and much business conversation is plagued with defensiveness, euphemism, and signs of insecurity.

In an open environment, the standard for all corporate communication is complete forthrightness. Everyone gets the same facts, the same explanation of larger context, and the same interpretation of information. A message is the same whether it is traveling up or down the ranks, or "sideways" to outside audiences who have their own primary interest in it.

How does the link between openness and credibility contribute to competitive advantage? First, openness encourages credibility because it ensures that everyone is getting the same information. Credibility, in turn, leads to trust, which is essential for enlisting the commitment of employees, customers, and suppliers—of anyone even remotely connected with the organization. Finally, high commitment undergirds superior business performance.

STUMBLING BLOCKS

Suppose for a moment that you have been developing an idea that you think could revolutionize the way your department functions. One day you bring it to your CEO. Before you even finish describing your plan, she cuts you off. "There are a lot of problems with that idea," she tells you. "It'll never work."

Or let's suppose that you are the manager, and one of your people brings his idea to you. As you listen, you become aware of several serious pitfalls. You want to appear open, however, so instead of discussing potential problems, you tell him it is a great idea and promise to think about it.

It is easy to see the lack of openness in the first example. In the second incident, it's much more subtle. Telling others what we think they want to hear instead of what we are really thinking may masquerade as consideration. But, in truth, it is grossly unfair, depriving them not only of feedback but also of the opportunity to explain further. When we decide, "She's not ready to hear this" or "He can't handle that," we are actually making a judgment. But what if our unilateral judgment is inaccurate? Unless others know what we are thinking, they cannot correct our misconceptions. And unless we get feedback, we fall into the trap of having our opinions become self-fulfilling prophecies.

The Gap between Theory and Practice

Perhaps the major threat to openness is the gap that can develop between what we believe (our espoused theory) and the message we send by our actions (our theory in practice). For example, we may say we believe that "honesty is the best policy," and yet find ourselves telling others what we think they want to hear instead of what we really think, as in the second example I have just given.

In our early discussions on openness at Hanover, Harvard professor Chris Argyris, a long-time student of learning and management teams, helped us understand how unaware people often are of the discrepancies between their espoused theory and their theory in action. Drawing on extensive research, Argyris demonstrated two models of human behavior:

Model 1 individuals have a strong drive to accomplish their own agendas. They strive to exert control over tasks. They maximize winning and minimize losing. Model 1 behavior creates an environment in which people have little freedom of choice, take few risks, and often make only a token commitment to the goals of the organization.

Model 2 individuals, on the other hand, design situations in which all the participants can use personal initiative and take responsibility for their actions. They believe in joint control of tasks. They consider the sharing of valid information essential to the capacity of both individuals and the organization to grow and learn. Model 2 behavior contributes to an environment in which people have significant freedom of choice, are committed to the goals of the organization, and are willing to take risks to further those goals.

Without an open environment, we are unlikely ever to discover the difference between what we do and what we say. But uncovering our hidden agendas and bringing our beliefs (what we say) and our actions (what we do) into harmony contributes to our personal growth, a positive working environment, and the success of our companies.

THE EFFECTIVENESS OF OPENNESS

All too often, there is a dichotomy between the objectives of an organization and the needs of its people. But openness contributes to a fundamental harmony between the two. Openness—especially when practiced with merit and localness—contributes to superior organizational performance. Decisions that result from an open discussion of the merits of a situation by the people closest to that situation are usually far more effective than decisions motivated by political or bureaucratic considerations.

Openness helps create an environment in which people are active participants—in which they use personal initiative, share ideas and insights, take responsibility for their actions, work together to achieve goals, and gain the satisfaction that comes from leaving their handprint on the organization.

Openness builds competitive advantage because it nurtures cooperation and stimulates the thinking and creativity of the people closest to the problems and the solutions. Equally important, openness combined with a spin-free corporate ecology has a crucial impact on the character, personality, spirit, and maturity of the individuals who spend years in such a work setting. Each of us journeys into our adulthood through a blending of three forces: our genetic inheritance, the exercise of our own will, and the environment. A work culture that reinforces truth, competent conversation, and an understanding of the connection between human work and purpose cannot help but achieve success.

Openness and Synergy

When informed people pool their ideas and talents to solve a problem or take advantage of an opportunity, they unleash the knowledge, experience, and abilities of everyone in the group. Decisions made in this way are often superior in two respects. First, discussions by a group usually bring out more information, insights, and points of view than are available to an individual. Second, people who participate in the discussion usually implement the decision with greater conviction than those who are simply following orders.

Even when not practiced perfectly, openness encourages us to express our ideas and gives us access to the ideas of others. It lets us know what is happening, why it is happening, and the thinking behind what is happening. It results in decisions that incorporate many viewpoints and experiences. It enhances our personal as well as our business relationships. It is a powerful contributor to a merit environment—one in which the search for the best solution takes precedence over other considerations.

VI.
LEANNESS

The values of localness, merit, and openness lie at the very heart of human maturity and growth. They are actually derived from three time-tested understandings about human nature. Localness, for example, is a version of freedom—the freedom to make our own decisions about the work that affects us the most. Merit is derived from concepts about responsibility and accountability. Openness has its roots in the virtue truth—and in living up to that virtue more fully than is customary in many organizational settings. Openness comes from the concept of honesty.

Leanness, or the wise stewardship of resources, is a fourth value—one that directly drives business performance.

OVERCOMING THE HABIT OF WASTE

We are all familiar with the ups and downs of the stock market. Since no one can regularly predict when an up market will turn down or when a down market will turn up, successful investors carefully choose stocks in companies they believe will, on average, perform better through both the up and the down phases of the investment cycle.

A friend of mine, an investment manager, puts it this way: Most stocks rise in an up market. Practically all stocks go down in a down market. But some stocks never go back up when the market again rises. He puts stocks in two categories: eggs and tennis balls. When the market drops, the eggs splatter and never rise. When the market drops, the tennis balls drop but rebound when the market rises. This manager carefully chooses the companies in which he invests on the basis of their ability to prepare themselves in up markets to handle down markets, so that when the market changes, they will bounce back.

Just as there is an investment cycle, there is a business cycle with ups and downs, and there is a life cycle with good times and bad times. Just as there is no way for an investor to predict when a down market will occur, there is even less likelihood that a business can avoid the down phase of a cycle or an individual can escape difficult times in life.

The key to successful investing, a successful business, or a successful personal life is how well we prepare ourselves to handle the down sides. Such preparation is best done during good times. When things are at their worst, it is often too late to prepare.

Many business historians tell us that the biggest mistakes take place during prosperity. Thomas J. Watson, founder of IBM, called prosperity "more dangerous for a business than depression." That statement's implication—that it is easier to be successful in bad times than in good ones—may seem preposterous on the surface. However, when I think about it, I find it consistent with my own experience.

In times of adversity we make few voluntary decisions. Circumstances and pressures dictate our choices. In good times, without the constraints and pressures imposed by adversity, we must rely on self-discipline and sound judgment.

Our human nature is flawed. Culture, founded in traditional values and virtues, is the primary force capable of augmenting our individual will so that we can pull our behavior up the moral ladder when the temptation to slide down is strong. By regularly inculcating values, virtues, and more enlightened practices throughout an organization, leaders help people respond at a higher level when they face the temptation to be expedient, to take shortcuts, to waste, to be hubristic, or to let standards slip.

The business scene is full of examples of companies that, intoxicated with profit and growth, allow euphoria to overcome common sense, experience, and rationality when economic conditions shift from a period of rising prosperity to a time of declining growth. It is easy to fall victim to excessively expansive thinking.

Not surprisingly, all of us have an appetite for ever-increasing comfort. Likewise, corporations have a hunger for growth and expansion. Trouble crops up when these appetites become excessive or ill timed, whether for an individual's financial capacity or for a corporation's capacity to remain stable during an economic downturn.

How does an organization avoid getting "fat" or overextending itself financially on the mistaken assumption that good times will last forever?

LEANNESS—A VALUE FOR ALL SEASONS

Leanness derives from thrift, which, throughout the history of civilization, has been an established virtue, while its opposite—waste and extravagance—are vices that weaken both cultures and individual character. As we often see in the workplace, unrestrained materialism will lead to moral and psychological corruption. Lavish spending by corporate higher-ups distorts their sense of values and distances them from their sense of obligation to colleagues and customers. It also engenders deep resentment and disillusionment among employees, thus lowering their commitment to the organization's mission. And this consumption will spread like a disease throughout the organization. Unfortunately, uncontrolled displays of opulence by senior executives, and the conversations attendant to them, get imitated and passed down through the managerial echelons, so that the prevailing focus becomes not "What's right?" but "What's in it for me?"

Even more damaging, excess materialism can lead to distorted decisions by business leaders. Imagine an executive who takes the corporate jet into a manufacturing town to fire people. In the name of economic competition, this kind of leader is inflicting all the sacrifice on the lower ranks while he lives the high life himself. The economic disparity between this executive and the rest of the ranks not only corrodes employee commitment but also isolates the executive from the results of his actions. Consequently, the company loses commitment, that essential ingredient for success. Further, any degree of openness is destroyed because the executive cannot see the unintended fallout from his behavior—fallout that eventually will loom as a much larger problem than anyone may have expected.

How else can we capture the essence of leanness? Let's begin by considering what it is not. Leanness is not cheapness. It is not paying low salaries or accepting shoddy work or inferior thinking. It is not understaffing. It is not locating offices in rundown buildings.

What, then, is leanness? It is demanding that every dollar we spend earn a high return for our company. It is being mindful that many business and financial mistakes arise from waste, extravagance, overspending, monument building, ostentation, unsound expansion, and other wrong-headed actions that can eventually become bad habits. Although unwise practices intensify during good times, their penalties usually strike in hard times.

Leanness is a frame of mind that helps a person or an organization grow and prosper in good times and bounce back from bad times. It is a way of life in which we base our sense of satisfaction on what we achieve, not on what we spend. A lean organization avoids spending for show because it knows that results and performance speak for themselves. It feels no compulsion to impress others. Furthermore, leanness must always be combined with efforts to improve quality. It is easy to be "lean" by doing things late and poorly, but it's not very satisfying. And it's no great feat to deliver timely and excellent service if a company is rolling in money, but it is a hard fact of life that dazzling profits don't continue forever.

Leanness is thus a future-oriented value, preparing the way for the inevitable bad times, strengthening moral excellence, and countering the tempting pull toward excess. More specifically, it offers three major benefits to those who practice it.

The First Benefit of Leanness:
Competitiveness as an Enterprise

Businesspeople have two constituencies:
1) customers who want value in proportion to what they spend for a product or service; and
2) owners who want a healthy return on their investment.

Leanness is a primary enabler of both these outcomes.

Leanness is at the heart of keeping an enterprise ahead of its competitors, particularly one that is in or is entering into the commodity phase of its life cycle. Leanness that is embedded in the culture and character of a company gives that company a competitive advantage over an organization that has to rely on accounting controls and budget constraints to fight waste.

The Second Benefit of Leanness:
Security

The capacity of a company to provide opportunities for each person as well as economic security in adverse times is derived from its ability to compete successfully in the marketplace. Leanness contributes to that successful competition, which, in turn, contributes to the quality of everyone's work-life over the long term.

When I read in the financial pages that Company X is laying off 10,000 people, or ten percent of its workforce, as the result of a recent slowdown in demand, my reaction runs along these lines: How can you accumulate 10,000 more people than you need? That's a small city! Haven't you noticed yourself getting fat? It is amazing how some large corporations lay off thousands of people in a single stroke, but won't lay off one at a time who may be superfluous or failing to meet standards. If you do not regularly weed the garden, the garden eventually becomes choked off by weeds. And when a company is careless in exercising its stewardship of human resources, the chances are that it has also been wasteful in its stewardship of material resources.

"Restructuring" has become a favorite business euphemism. When a company announces a restructuring, it is frequently admitting that five or ten years earlier, its management made some economically flawed decisions, often leaving its current managers with little choice. If they do not cut back, they risk watching the entire enterprise go under. Today's restructuring is the price of yesterday's folly. Tomorrow's restructuring will be caused by today's excesses.

Leanness is the value that underlies management's responsibility for the stewardship of resources.

The Third Benefit of Leanness: Personal Growth

Perhaps the most important payoff from leanness is what it does for our personal growth. We live in a self-indulgent society. We have carried labor-saving devices all the way to the electric toothbrush. We have pills for the most minor discomforts. And we have portable TVs, radios, and computers to distract us from knowing and living with ourselves.

The result is that we are dependent on external conditions to feel good, even while our spirits are starved for the nourishment that comes from being independent, self-reliant, and capable of identifying with and contributing to a larger cause.

Unfortunately, the excesses involved in indulging ourselves and seeking the quick and easy way have come to be seen as the norm, while a sense of personal responsibility, appropriate austerity, and corporate mission are often seen as old-fashioned. But I believe we grow stronger by placing constructive restraints on our appetites, by making constructive demands on our capacities, and by undertaking a lifelong search to find better ways to do our work. That's what leanness is all about.

Part 3

LEADERSHIP
PRINCIPLES

*Most people, regardless of their level of
education, have within them a built-
in horse manure detector (HMD),
just as they have a mind, a soul, and
a spirit.*

VII.
A VALUES-BASED, VISION-DRIVEN CULTURE

A PARABLE

International Financial (IF) has created a vision called "Top Quality," which consists of three parts: a service improvement program, an introduction of redesigned work processes, and a delivery strategy to reach more and better customers. Its objective is to make the company the first choice of its customers, employees, and investors. Around this vision the bank's senior executives expect to transform their culture in a way that more fully engages the minds and spirits of their employees to enhance the company's financial performance and market share.

Stanton Ivory, the Executive Vice President, is boldly spearheading the vision movement. He is quoted in a recent internal publication as saying, "There's going to be only one kind of person in this company. We want people who are committed, who are on-board, who are part of the team, and who buy into the vision wholeheartedly. I'm going to see this through. I started the IF Top Quality Vision, and I will ensure that it comes to fruition."

Certainly, what management hopes the vision will achieve is desirable. Yet this vision is not likely to inspire the majority of employees who do the ordinary work upon which the company's performance depends. Why not?

A Vision Can't Be Sold

IF's Top Quality Vision is a package of programs and slogans that is being implemented as a project to be merchandised to employees in the same way one might sell soap for better personal hygiene to people aspiring to the next level of social class. The human resources department pushes all this through with training manuals and coffee mugs. Just in case some employees find the sales pitch resistible, there is also a dose of economic coercion. Insightful, street-smart employees soon conclude that the purpose of the vision is to get them to work harder, smarter, and cooperatively so the company has better financial performance and the senior executives look better in the eyes of their board. The vision is intended to convince employees to do what Ivory wants them to do because Ivory knows what is best for them.

Judging from Ivory's pronouncement, the vision in this company is seen as a mechanical tool to get done what top management wants to get done. Later, Ivory expresses impatience at the pace with which managers in the ranks accept his vision, and he complains that the employees just don't realize that a stronger company will actually benefit them in the future.

Three Important Principles

Why is the Top Quality Vision likely to fail? A corporate vision that genuinely energizes its employees is not some magical picture of the future that is conceived by the boss and then injected into each person through meetings, discussions, slogans, and the brandishing of carrots and sticks. Visions that energize the individual must have three important principles:

+ They must be aspirational.
+ They must be intensely personal.
+ They must be internalized.

Aspirations

Just as people need oxygen to breathe and thus support their physical life, they need aspirations to enjoy emotional health. Highly energized, forward-looking companies are distinguished not by a carefully worded corporate vision articulated by the CEO, but by an environment where each person can pursue vocational and organizational aspirations. An individual aspiration is related to one's career, but a corporate aspiration has to do with the kind of organization the larger entity wants to become. The "larger entity" is not necessarily the whole corporation, but the universe to which the employee directly belongs, such as a division, region, or local branch. The objective is not to inoculate each level in sequence with the vision of the top level of executives, but to awaken and nourish the natural appetite of employees for vocational aspirations toward improving the organization to which they devote two-thirds of their waking lives. The objective is to stimulate those in ordinary jobs to apply their spirit, creativity, ingenuity, and thinking toward making their company the best it can be. Only when this aspiration is internalized can employees express their personalities and develop their talents so they can become more than they are today.

Personalization

The second principle, often overlooked, is that the kind of vision that energizes a person's vocational life is intensely personal. My vision for myself gets me out of bed each morning with eager anticipation to go to work in order to build what I want to achieve. It doesn't do anything for anyone else's level of energy or inspiration. Naturally, if I succeed in building what I want to achieve—for example, a higher quality of customer service—and if it enriches the company, I expect a fair reward. Only to the extent that I can personally identify with my organization and its mission, and only to the extent that I can see my organization as an extension of myself, will I fully commit myself to its goals.

Internalization

The third principle of shaping culture around visions and values is that for visions to be inspiring, they must be internalized by the employees. People have to make the company vision their own—and this takes time. An executive attempting to force a fixed vision on an organization in a short period of time enters perilous waters. The vision needs testing by the people for its appropriateness for the organization and themselves. The executive who pushes too hard risks being met with unhealthy organizational responses, such as resistance, passivity, and lack of individual initiative.

Any leader who sets out to transform an organization's culture ought to begin with a healthy dose of humility. It is not unlike matching the right-sized nut to a bolt. If you mismatch the sizes and try to force them together, you strip the threads and ruin both the nut and the bolt. The task of the senior executive in large corporations, where decisions and activities are widely dispersed, is not to define "The Vision" and then try to force-fit it into the echelons of the organization through salesmanship or coercion. Instead, it begins with cultivating a personal vision for one's self and one's company. This task is a lonely job that takes time and requires reflective insight into one's self, one's corporation, its industry, and its surrounding society.

If you are a leader, you cannot build an effective program around your own conclusions; you have to explain your ideas and beliefs about what the organization should stand for and its central strategic direction to a variety of respected people who have a stake in the organization, so they may test your ideas. Out of this process, you sharpen your own aspirations for the company and begin a dialogue about visions and aspirations.

The task at hand is to create an environment where aspirations flow through every sector of the company, and all employees breathe in a climate that nourishes their appetite for aspirations. The CEO leads the visionary process by demonstrating his or her own vision and inspiring others to conceive and live up to their own visions for their own areas of responsibility.

CREATING A VISION

How does one go about conceiving one's vision for a particular area of responsibility? Although there is no single formula for doing so, here are three questions that have helped me over the years.

Question 1: What are our organizational roots?

On many occasions, I have seen troubled companies recruit an outside manager from a highly successful competitor. The new manager immediately tries to replicate the culture and strategies of her former company. Frequently, she recruits a number of her former colleagues to her new employer.

I have never seen a great corporation emerge from efforts to copy another company. Why? Because the leader usually fails to ground his or her visions by connecting them to the roots of the corporation he or she is leading. Each generation of management stands on the shoulders of every previous generation of workers and managers. Through indifference to the past, the new leader condemns as worthless the life's work of those he or she is charged with inspiring. That is not an auspicious beginning for earning voluntary followership. Further, the imported executive is abdicating one of a leader's most important responsibilities—to provide context so that members of the organization can decide for themselves if the new direction is sound. Otherwise, the people are likely to adopt a wait-and-see attitude, suspecting the vision might be just a passing fad.

Organizational transformations do not occur simply because the boss wants them and thinks he has the power to coerce others to commit to the same course of action. Transformations occur because those in ordinary jobs grasp the intellectual reasons for change and then internalize a commitment to pursue those changes. Commitments are born out of convictions, which, in turn, are always derived from voluntary choice and not from a direct order. And amplifying context around the organization's roots is one of a leader's tools for building the internalized convictions and commitments that underlie transformation.

Question 2: What is the current reality of our organization?

I approach this question by looking at the corporation from both the inside and the outside. It is important to do both, and probably at the same time. If you skip looking from the inside perspective, you might erect your externally focused vision on a foundation unable to support it. But if you skip the outside perspective, the culture will tend toward narcissism, chauvinism, and insularity, and will fail to adequately test reality.

When examining your organization from the inside, look for what functions well and what does not. Analyze the organization's ecology for decision making and action. What are the influences? Which are tacit and which are explicit? The power of your vision will be directly related to your insight in assessing the current reality—not as analyzed by management, but as seen by the worker assembling the product on the factory floor, or by the customer at the point of trying to get a problem resolved, or by a front-line supervisor trying to sell the boss on making a change to improve departmental effectiveness. You know your view of current reality is hitting the proverbial nail on the head when an experienced employee on the front line has an "aha!" reaction and responds with vigorous agreement.

Obtaining an insightful external appraisal of your organization is relatively uncomplicated. Ask several customers, distributors, and vendors to describe and rank your organization against selected competitors. The vendors may need extra reassurance that you want their criticism as well as their praise, and that they will not lose your favor by being candid. Ask your financial people to compare your organization's performance with the top ten companies in your industry.

Also, get a comparison with industry as a whole, since your entire industry may have developed arteriosclerotic myths that blind it to industry forces.

The objective in addressing these two questions is to get an inside and an outside description of unvarnished reality for your area of responsibility. The summation should be free from exaggeration or biases. Resist temptation to use spin. We want people to judge the substance of the assessment and make their own conclusions.

Question 3: What ought to be?

Work should be a vehicle for growing innate capacities, for maturing, for enjoying friendship, for exercising a sense of purpose, and for earning a livelihood. But if that were all work did, it would be an incomplete and narcissistic endeavor. Work is also how we make our contribution to the community and the world.

Whenever I noodle about "what ought to be" for an economic activity in which I'm engaged, I try to be mindful of two distinct dimensions—the aspirational and the inspirational. At the same time, I try to remain grounded and realistic.

Aspiration is looking up and looking ahead. It is the organization becoming better tomorrow than it is today in any number of spheres, such as maturity, reputation, reliability, and quality.

Inspiration is a psychic fuel that engages people because of the nobility or innate goodness of what it is they are pursuing. There's an old story about a boy who goes up to a workman and asks, "What are you doing?" The man says, "Laying brick." A little further on, the boy finds another workman and asks the same question. "Building a wall," the man answers. Then the boy finds a third man and asks the question, "What are you doing?" The man answers, "I'm building a great cathedral."

Isn't the art of coaxing "what ought to be" from within ourselves and others the same journey the boy took from "laying bricks" to "building a great cathedral"?

In societies built around free markets, businesses can best measure their external performance by how well they combine creating wealth and increasing market share over a long period of time. Profits measure how efficiently the organization uses capital; growth tells how effectively the organization is satisfying customers. The words "over a long period of time" are important, for in short periods of time, luck, cycles, fads, and the use of accounting tricks often distort business results.

Whether they run a global conglomerate, a division, or a modest-sized self-standing business unit, executives have a responsibility to think through and articulate the "what ought to be" dimension of their vision for their area of responsibility. It should wed inspirational conditions that enhance the human development of their constituents with goals for business performance that are constructively stretching but also realistic. And, of course, the best foundation from which to discover what ought to be is a deep understanding and appreciation of the entity's roots and an insightful reading of current reality.

ENLISTING SUPPORT

When I had occasion to go through this process at Hanover Insurance, I was careful not to anoint my vision the "corporate vision." Instead, when I spoke to employees about my vision for the company, I encouraged them to think about it, to test it, and if they had concerns or ideas, to tell me. When they did, I listened and let them know they were heard. I also told them that it is not my vision that is important, except for me; but it is their visions for themselves, their people, and their areas of responsibility that really count. The day that an individual gets out of bed to build what he wants to achieve, instead of because he has to be at work by eight o'clock, is a transformational day in the life of that person. Furthermore, if, in my company, only ten percent of the people cross that transformational line, and if, in our competitor's company, only five percent have crossed it, then our company has a significant competitive advantage that will be reflected in better business performance. When we have thirty percent of our people crossing that line, we will have built an overwhelming advantage. Again, what is important in corporate cultural transformation is not the exact content of visions, but rather the process of getting individual aspirations to flower in every corner of the organization.

People internalize aspirations and visions through combining reflection and experience. That is why staff meetings intended to discuss and draft a corporate or departmental vision invariably fail to come up with inspiring ideas that go beyond agreeable platitudes. The moment we cast visioning as something "for the organization" as opposed to being "mine," the passion, which is the source of inspiration and aspiration, dissipates. A visionary company is an organization where lots of people have aspirations and future-focused mental models, not a company with a carefully crafted vision statement. I counsel leaders who want to have vision at the center of their culture to begin by composing their own vision for their enterprise and then invite their employees to test their ideas, and, better yet, to weave vision into ordinary business conversation.

Leaders must be careful never to cross the line from inspiration to manipulation in using visions or values to foster cultural transformation. I am not talking about being good at masking manipulative intentions with a veneer of sincerity. Instead, I mean extinguishing every bit of manipulative inclination from both your character and your style. The antidote to manipulation is an unwavering commitment to truth and forthrightness and to asking people to do only that which is purposeful toward achieving the highest common interest of the enterprise.

NURTURING A VISION

The first step of the journey is to know yourself and to seek greater alignment between who you are, what you believe about humans, and what you do in practice. The second step is to understand and connect with your entity's roots, whether this entity is a department or the entire corporation. Then assess current reality as if you were a detached observer. Do it from both an inside and outside perch, and concentrate on where your product or service is made, performed, or sold. Finally, think through what you believe "ought to be" by drawing on your knowledge and experience about industry competitive conditions, social aspirations, human nature, human values, and human needs.

I suggest you design two dimensions to your vision, one inspirational and the other in terms of measurable business performance. A wise man once said that man does not live by bread alone.

Don't try to sell your vision or inoculate anyone with it. Just talk about it, letting your natural enthusiasm flow. Ask others to test it, and honestly and nonjudgmentally hear them out. It will get better as you go along.

After you have set the example, ask others to think seriously about their aspirations for their sections of responsibility. While you may not have an exuberant breakthrough moment, when an inspiring vision appears, you will find that, over time, you'll begin to recognize a visionary dimension to discussions about ordinary business activities. Other people will begin to say that your folks know where they are headed and what they stand for.

FIGURE 2. TWO DIMENSIONS OF VISION

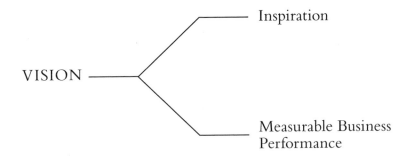

THE END OF THE PARABLE

International Financial is trying to adopt a theory of governance in which visions and values exert more influence in guiding decisions than do individual executive inclinations to command and control. That is, I believe, the appropriate direction for guiding an enterprise through the twenty-first century. The challenge is ensuring that the implementation methods are congruent with the theories of governance.

Before Stanton Ivory can change his corporation, he must change himself. He must actually compose his own vision, and it must be of sufficient quality and depth to attract voluntary followership. It must be connected to his values. He must understand that a vision is not a mechanical tool to get people to do what he wants. Instead, the task he faces is to unleash the pent-up energies within the company's employees by nourishing their aspirations for vocational fulfillment in a way that enhances International Financial's business imperatives of profit, growth, and customer satisfaction.

A vision-driven and values-based culture concerns not just matters of the head but matters of the heart; not just matters of profit but matters of soul—in short, it concerns the very essence of our humanity.

VIII.
THE MORAL FORMATION
OF MANAGERS

THE HORSE MANURE DETECTOR/HMD FACTOR

When I was a private in the U.S. Army Infantry in the 1950s, I was puzzled why one company commander inspired remarkable loyalty from his troops and high commitment to our unit's mission, while under his successor, morale and performance plummeted to the bottom of regimental rankings in less than six months. The army is an extraordinary laboratory for studying the impact of character on the effectiveness of leaders because so many of the other factors that influence organizational performance are standardized. For example, all privates in the same line of work get identical training, follow the same standardized operating procedures, and get the same pay. Why did performance differ so markedly between my two company commanders, both of whom had graduated from West Point?

Captain Driesenstock, the captain who inspired loyalty and high performance, was soft-spoken, short in stature, and highly respected by his men. He always leveled with us, telling us when our performance was good and when it was poor. He treated us with respect and fairness, and protected us from the chicken excrement that regularly comes down from regimental staff. We knew he was committed to us and to our unit's mission.

His successor was six feet two inches tall, possessed a deep resonant voice, and was a casting director's dream of what an army commander ought to look like. Unfortunately, his performance didn't accord with his look. It took only a few exercises over a period of a couple of months for the lowest private (me) and everyone else to figure out that we were being used to advance his career. Decisions were made to impress higher-ups, not to accomplish sensible military imperatives, and chicken excrement from the regimental staff usually hit us (and not him) full blast.

How did the troops so quickly distinguish between authentic leadership and the counterfeit version? I have mulled over this question many times throughout my business career because the situation repeats itself so often in corporate life. The troops spot the fakers quickly, while it takes years for the General to catch on. I think it is easier to spot a leader's serious character weaknesses from the bottom than it is from the top because aspiring pseudo leaders put a lot of energy into impressing higher echelons and less into putting integrity into their relationships with the people for whom they are responsible.

I have also come to this conclusion: Most people, regardless of their level of education, have within them a built-in HMD, just as they have a mind, a soul, and a spirit—none of which can be identified on an anatomy chart. The HMD helps individuals sort out whether they are receiving an honest, forthright communication or one that is intended to manipulate their behavior. The HMD helps to sort out whether an action is taken for the sake of everyone or just out of self-interest.

As we know, spin control takes different forms. Sometimes exaggeration is used to slant a subject a certain way; sometimes anxiety or fear is used to push opinion in a certain direction; at other times information is withheld to influence decision making. Most of us can't articulate how our HMD works, but we intuitively decide not to commit to propositions that trigger the alarm. Thus, the manipulative boss gets pseudo followership in response to pseudo leadership. That is why executive moral formation should be grounded in a passionate commitment to truth, forthrightness, and respect for the capacity in ordinary people to discern between high- and low-quality propositions.

Over the short term, a manager may temporarily achieve his goals by manipulating people. He might then conclude that manipulation works. It does not. In a manipulated relationship, the highest price is paid by the person who does the manipulating, for he dilutes his own capacity to recognize truth and sincerity, even in himself. It is human nature to see the rest of the world through who we are. If we are manipulators, we lose the capacity to know when someone else is being honest and forthright. The manipulator may win a few events, but he often tarnishes his reputation and ruins any chance that his troops will look up to him. Conversely, transformational leaders are highly sensitive to the vibrations from their own HMD and respect its presence in everyone else.

Manipulated employees can pay a painful price. Those who do not consciously recognize the horse manure often join in the pursuit of illusions. Their subsequent depression, bitterness, and other symptoms often get attributed to "personality," when, in fact, they are often the indirect result of diseased cultures and flawed supervision. Burnout is not caused by hard work as much as it is by working in dysfunctional cultures.

HUMAN CAPITAL DRIVES FINANCIAL CAPITAL

"We judge others by what they do; we judge ourselves by our intentions."
"What you do thunders so loud, I can't hear what you say."

These two quotations, one from an anonymous author and the other from Henry David Thoreau, are a succinct summary of the difficulties of changing an organization from one that is considered ordinary by present standards to one that aspires to practice moral excellence. The practice of moral excellence requires more than avoiding what is illegal, or simply conforming to contemporary commercial ethical principles. It requires us, in addition, to pursue moral truths with the same vigor and commitment we bring to technological, marketing, and financial achievement.

Why make such an investment in moral excellence? There is a deeply embedded assumption in many management cultures that living up to top-tier moral expectations is not compatible with earning superior financial returns. This is an impoverished view of both human nature and the marketplace. It needs to be changed.

The psychological fuel that energizes human beings has several general sources, including, for example, fear, greed, ideology, the pursuit of moral excellence, and love. None of us is driven by a single fuel—we all run on a mixture. But the higher the proportion of moral excellence and love in the mixture, the better the performance of the organization. Fear and greed cause counterproductive side effects. Fear drives out creativity, initiative, and cooperation. Greed puts self-interest ahead of the common interest and causes fragmentation.

Conversely, the pursuit of moral excellence is the most effective, enduring, and elevating path to energizing organizations because it taps into our enduring appetites for truth, learning, honesty, purposefulness, and love. As a byproduct, it engenders a social ecology that fosters individual growth, maturation, and happiness.

Are such aspirations too idealistic? I don't believe so. While perfection in moral behavior is never achievable, the energy we seek to release and the inner happiness we desire are derived from pursuing moral excellence and love in a community with shared ideals, while achieving a level of practice that exceeds both our past efforts and our competitors' present ones. In other words, performance improvements are achieved by getting better, not by being perfect.

On the other hand, there are serious downside consequences of not pursuing moral excellence. What begins as exaggerated advertising, or a shoddy product from cutting corners, or a promise that you know you are unlikely to fulfil eventually corrupts a culture to the extent that employees also become disenchanted, losing their appetite to buy into the organization's mission. That not only impacts profits unfavorably, but it also jeopardizes survival.

MORAL FORMATION: A DIFFICULT JOURNEY

If pursuing moral excellence is a superior method for driving business performance, why do we find it at the core of so few companies? Moral excellence requires commitments that run counter to many habits and mores in Western society, especially such habits as going for instant gratification rather than working for lifetime satisfaction, seeking technological solutions rather than developing qualities associated with the human spirit, and looking good rather than being good.

Though some recognize and lament the character imperfections that infect the ranks of large authoritarian hierarchies, they seem paralyzed when it comes to doing anything about them. One reason for this is the systems principle of delay between cause and effect. In other words, when the lag time between an act and its visible penalty is long, we do not clearly associate the two. But if smoking on Monday gave you cancer on Tuesday, few would smoke. Thus, rather than rooting out the infection of low moral behavior, people adapt to it by becoming political, bureaucratic, and adept at the kind of corporate lingo that may be accurate but is seldom purposeful.

Most employees want to be moral. They prefer to spend their working lives in moral environments. Most company leaders, including members of the board of directors and the CEO, want their organizations to be moral. Then why is living up to high moral practices so difficult? There are three reasons.

First, after decades of being treated as a herd of hired hands (even if this treatment is compassionate and fair), employees are highly skeptical of new schemes of governance. They say to themselves and their close colleagues, "I hear what management says, but do they mean it? Will they personally practice what they advocate—will they, for example, tighten their own belts in a program to lower overhead? Will my boss zero in on our real problems and not be obsessed with the politics of every situation? Can I say what I really think about our critical issues without being labeled a troublemaker?"

Second, corporations have not undertaken major efforts to develop philosophical and moral underpinnings for governing their people. What most have is a hodgepodge of notions that come from Roman army ideas about control, from technological innovations to maximize the efficiency of mass production, from scientific principles about measurements, and from the latest management fads. This is not enough to keep thousands of people engaged in a competitive, complex undertaking on an upward trajectory over generations.

Corporations, to excel and endure, need philosophy and doctrine just as do religions, sovereign nations, and educational institutions. If the United States did not have its Constitution, Bill of Rights, the Federalist Papers, and patriotic traditions, would it have overcome all our crises—slavery, the World Wars, the Great Depression, Watergate, the close 2000 presidential election, the terrorist attacks—and gone on to endure and prosper? Ought not a business institution that engages thousands of people and billions of assets and that affects lots of lives have a philosophy tailored to its mission to give it guidance and inspiration through good and bad times?

Third, managers have received minimal instruction and guidance about the moral dimension of exercising their responsibilities. Moral excellence must be undergirded by a network of managers who have paid attention to their own formation as human beings—a subject seldom found in the curriculum of our corporate management education programs or in the business schools, even in so-called "corporate ethics" programs. My observations persuade me that the most influential forces on managerial moral practices are parenting, mentoring, high school education, and the example of senior executives.

Although the difficulties are daunting, think for a moment of what might be achieved. The competitive advantage for those organizations would be breathtaking. The potential in releasing bottled-up human energy is twofold: a high percentage increase in productivity, and an unimagined improvement in relationships with external constituencies, who will respond positively to the quality of the experiences they have with such an organization.

How does one begin the arduous task of retrofitting a corporation's culture to put the pursuit of moral excellence at its core? For me, the task would begin by facing the character disorders that affect human relations in routine business activities in a manager's area of responsibility. How are decisions influenced by political connivance? To what degree do actions, intended to maximize self-interest, interfere with achieving the company's overall interest? Does bureaucracy overwhelm individual responsibility? Do rules and procedures always take precedence over human judgment, even when everybody knows that the application of the rule to a particular situation is counterproductive or unjust? Do accepted corporate lies deaden the spirit of inquiry?

Viewing Responsibility on a Moral Stepladder

In my experience as a CEO, the essence of transforming an organization's character begins with raising the level of managerial moral behavior in routine matters that are usually invisible to anyone outside a small number of people in a given manager's immediate work environs. One way to grasp the abstract notion of "raising the level of moral behavior" is to envision a stepladder for ranking a manager's response to an ordinary day-to-day business situation.

For instance, an employee suggests to his manager that a certain standard procedure is wasteful and might be performed more economically by a proposed change. But the manager believes that such a change, while beneficial to the company, would be unpopular with the head of another department who, in turn, would lobby against it with his boss. So he decides to ignore the suggestion because he believes it is better for his own interest. In other words, by deciding in this case to avoid risk, he puts self-interest ahead of common interest and ahead of his personal responsibility. The consequences of this innocuous-appearing decision is to weaken the fiber of his own character and stifle the appetite of employees to commit their initiative and spirit to the corporation.

The scenario I have described represents behavior on a low rung of the moral stepladder. If it were investigated, it would probably be excused as something that fell between the cracks. In fact, incidents similar to it are everyday events in most companies and government departments. No headline-grabbing moral transgression occurred. No illegal act happened, nor can anyone point with evidence to a lie. Probably no company procedure was violated. But acts like this, repeated over and over again, sap the vitality of worker teams, stunt the growth of individual aspiration, and tarnish the souls of corporations. And they damage financial performance as well because it is impossible for dispirited people to fully thrust themselves into productive action for the benefit of an organization of which they are—whether they admit it to themselves or not—ashamed. This rung of the moral stepladder could be labeled *legal but repugnant.*

On the next higher rung of the moral stepladder, the manager evaluates the employee's suggestion on the basis of how it would af-

FIGURE 3. THE MORAL STEPLADDER

Marching to
One's Full
Moral Potential

Moral Effort
Overwhelmed
by the System

Legal but
Repugnant

fect quality and cost. In this example, the manager isn't influenced by self-interest or politics, and he eventually recommends the idea. He may be surprised—the idea may be adopted—but more likely his original fears were accurate, and the suggestion is vetoed for political reasons. He advises the employee who originally made the suggestion and expresses appreciation for his thought and effort. I label this rung, *a moral effort overwhelmed by the system.*

The next higher rung on our ladder belongs to the manager whose sense of personal responsibility is becoming stronger. He attempts to change the basis of "the system" from politics to merit. How might he go about this? He could commit himself to adopting the highest rung on the ladder as his personal standard for his area of responsibility. Then he could set expectations for his staff that all departmental decisions be executed at the higher step of the ladder. After an example is set in his own department, which no doubt others will notice, he can credibly advocate for change in the larger entity. I call this step on our moral stepladder *marching to my full moral potential without becoming a fanatic or martyr.*

To say that transforming a corporation's character requires advancing the moral formation of its managers is not to imply that the majority of, or even many, managers are immoral. That has not been my experience in more than thirty-five years in corporate life. In fact, the opposite is true. Most of my colleagues (and adversaries) have been reasonably moral people. It is simply that the traditional command-and-control corporate structure depersonalizes work and, in many instances, substitutes material principles for moral values without understanding the human or financial consequences. Also, the natural human tendency toward self-justification leads to our having a "tin ear" for the moral tones of decisions and courses of actions.

Morality is either facilitated or hindered by the environment. People who may be moral at home are often less moral at work because only the most courageous of us can step out of roles and expectations when others sell out. The corporation should make it easier to act morally on its behalf by telling its people explicitly to "do the right thing." Again, we see that the journey toward moral excellence en-tails an ongoing ratcheting-up of our personal moral formation in tan-dem with creating a culture that supports and expects such practices. Climbing the moral stepladder is as necessary for transforming insti-tutional culture as using a hammer and saw is for building a house.

NO NEED TO INVENT NEW MORAL THEORIES

Although advancing the moral formation of managers sounds like a formidable task, fortunately, we don't need to invent new princi-ples and then wait a decade to see if they work. Much wisdom that has been collected and tested over the centuries can be tailored for the twentieth-century corporate and civil settings. The teachers who have helped me most are: Plato, Moses, Jesus, Adam Smith, Teil-hard de Chardin, Douglas McGregor, E. F. Schumacher, Jack Adam, Peter Senge, and Scott Peck. No doubt you have your own list of people who shaped your character. The challenge is not to come up with a master list of moralists and their theories, but rather to take what we already know and rigorously apply it to day-to-day mana-gerial conduct.

Transforming the moral ecology of a corporation, therefore, en-tails two broad-gauge strategies:

✦ Promulgating the four moral principles around which human relations are centered—localness, merit, openness, and lean-ness—in much the same way that financial information is centered on accounting principles.

✦ Encouraging managers to pursue their personal moral for-mation with the same vitality with which they develop pro-fessional skills. Personal moral formation begins with our attitudes toward virtue and vice. Shaping these attitudes re-quires us to examine ideas and to internalize beliefs that should be taken seriously because they have a profound effect on our lives. And because these attitudes are at the root of the "meaning of life," it is important that we don't unthinkingly accept the attitudes we have inherited or accidentally adopted. To qualify for leading people at any level in a first-rate company, a manager should be required to have paid serious attention to his or her moral formation and, consequently, to the construction of interior attitudes. When companies forgive corrupt conduct on the part of senior managers, they destroy all hope of establishing a moral foundation for their employees.

One of my implicit assumptions is that each of us possesses a will that is free to choose moral attitudes. Put differently, moral attitudes are not the same as being born left-handed. Though influenced by our environment, we each have a free will for making moral choices, which is developed through reason and discipline. The essence of our character is the moral dimension of all the acts and decisions that constitute our life to date.

CHOOSING THE HIGH ROAD

Imagine a recent college graduate setting out on a journey to reach lifetime happiness. He heads west on Route 90 and soon comes to a junction in the road that presents a choice. The sign for the road to the left says, "To Lifetime Happiness via Wealth and Power." The sign for the road to the right says, "To Lifetime Happiness via Virtue and Wisdom." The heavy traffic steers toward the wealth-and-power road. Its rewards are apparent, visible, appealing, and achievable over the short term. Many of the people who run our institutions today seem to have come down this road. Besides, most of our friends head in this direction.

What about the road that goes by way of virtue and wisdom? The dictionary defines virtue as "moral excellence; right living; goodness." Virtue comes from the Latin word *virtus*, which means manliness, or virility. Yet, in modern management circles, virtue is often associated with notions of softness and weakness—even though there is nothing soft about transforming typical corporate rat races into morally uplifting cultures that earn superior financial returns. This task requires an inner toughness of its leaders, a willingness to stand against the crowd, an ability to question well-rationalized assumptions, and a faith in the power of the human spirit.

Wisdom, in turn, is more than intelligence. It suggests a special quality of judgment in human affairs based on knowledge of moral principles, human nature, human needs, and human values. Wisdom is more than what people know, it is who they have become; and who they have become is determined by how congruent their behavior is with their knowledge. It is not enough for leaders to know moral principles—to have credibility as leaders and thus to earn followership, they must live up to their knowledge.

If you aspire to be a leader, the choice between the two roads is not easy. Within all of us, there is a pressure to go down the popular road. If, however, you assess this choice by asking yourself, "What kind of leader would I prefer for the company to which I am committing my career?" the answer is easy. Obviously, as a follower in an organization, you would prefer to have your environment designed and governed under the guidance of a leader whose driving influences are virtue and wisdom as opposed to power and wealth.

For some reason, pursuing the practice of corporate virtue, as I have described it, is seen as a trade-off against profitability. Nothing could be further from reality. Lowering acceptable standards of performance for technical business activities does not advance virtue, wisdom, or happiness. In fact, it does exactly the opposite. The path to happiness via virtue and wisdom is a demanding one. It stretches people. It raises energy levels. It strengthens commitments.

Many managers underachieve, not because they don't have any core beliefs, but because their core philosophies of life are underdeveloped. They simply have not devoted enough time to reading and reflecting on how the wisdom of the ages applies to their professional responsibilities. Is this not to be expected in a society where public education is value-neutral, organized religion has lost influence, family structure has been weakened, and the principal influence on young people's character is often television and motion pictures?

Perhaps, as corporations learn to understand the importance of the human spirit in achieving superior economic performance, enlightened corporate governance will also have a significant role to play in elevating the quality of life in the twenty-first century. The next generation of corporate managers could play a leading role in a societal transformation through reintroducing the moral dimension to everyday commerce—but if so, they will have to begin by learning how to shape their own interior dimensions.

The hardest part of managerial formation is the application of age-old moral wisdom and practice to issues that often infect the culture of modern enterprises. Some symptoms of a gap between wisdom and action that quickly come to mind are worker depersonalization ("I feel like a number around here."); institutional rigidity ("We can't change fast enough to keep up with innovation in our market."); and ineffective implementation of grand strategy ("It sounded like a winning strategy, but in the complexities of execution we made some incredibly poor judgments."). At the root of each of these symptoms is a virus called "hoarding power." Each level of management practices "trickle-down dispersal of authority." In my experience, it is worse at lower echelons than at higher ones. Not only is authority rationed, but so is information. Information on job techniques is readily available, but knowledge about context, which is necessary in order to handle the unanticipated, is scarce. By not sharing context, bosses keep workers dependent.

LOCALNESS AND THE MORAL STEPLADDER

Localness liberates us from the oppressive features of the command-and-control structure, so that all of us may use our jobs to fully develop ourselves and improve the organization's productivity. But how does this value work in practice when it comes to the moral formation of managers? How, for example, ought a manager at the fourth echelon from the CEO treat someone reporting directly to him who happens to be at the fifth echelon?

A quick and easy answer might be: "Like he treats everybody else, including his boss at the third echelon." That is a great answer, but few, in my estimation, live up to it. In fact, one of the best ways to read people's character is to compare their upward behavior with how they treat those who report to them. It can be quite revealing. Yes, two-facedness is a moral (though not a mortal) deficiency. When you think about it, the people who work for a manager have more impact on what he or she accomplishes than do those to whom that manager reports. Then why are people so often toadying to those above them and indifferent to those who are below? It has a lot to do with the way the system treats power, and much to do with our moral development.

Leaders who intend to build corporations that tap into the full inner resources of their people must pay as much attention to their own moral formation and that of their key managers as they do to mental and technical proficiency. That means that as an individual assumes more responsibility and rises up the ladder, moral formation becomes more important. The pure technical decisions usually all get resolved several echelons down in the organization. But leadership goes beyond rational decision making. The depth of commitment that an employee makes to his employer's well-being is directly related to his perception of the moral formation of his boss and his boss's bosses. The same can be said to a lesser degree about a customer's loyalty to a supplier.

Often, when a leader loses his position of power because his followers reject him, as happened to Richard Nixon, or when a board of directors removes a CEO because the company doesn't respond to his direction, those who have known the deposed individual over a long period of time frequently say, "Success didn't change him, it unmasked him." Behind that comment is the assumption that all along the road to high responsibility, the individual had some chinks in his character that people close to him knew about, even though he performed in a way that enabled him to move to even higher office. Minor cracks in the moral formation of those in middle management positions can be fatal flaws in those with senior management responsibilities.

This is a critical point that is often underestimated by those with the responsibility for anointing senior executives or CEOs and by those preparing themselves for higher responsibility. Will the potential leader—when temptation is strongest and no one seems to be looking—choose truth over fudging an answer to avoid looking bad, choose the common good of the enterprise over self-interest, and treat people on the factory floor with the same respect as those in the boardroom? There usually is no clear answer to this kind of question, but asking it does sharpen one's insight and intuition about the character of prospective leaders and their "size"—in other words, whether the person is big enough for the job.

ATTENTION TO PERSONAL GROWTH

Executive leadership generally means exercising power. This is true no matter where on the spectrum between command-and-control or servant leadership an individual chooses to operate. Generative leadership means exercising the kind of power in which constituents of the leader experience personal growth. Most people, in the course of their life, have had bosses or teachers who have influenced them to become more mature and capable. Likewise, many of us have had bosses and teachers under whose influence we failed to grow, or even deteriorated. I hesitate to call those teachers or managers degenerative, but it is at least fair to describe them as non-generative. Generative leaders are a mixture of servant and commander in style—but their driving force is not their style. It is, instead, their respect and caring for others, their maturity, their fidelity to truth, their openness, their courage, their constant pursuit of learning, and their willingness to subordinate personal interest to the good of the whole.

Generative leaders must advance in their own growth because both growth and decay are contagious. That is why corporations have a near-sacred responsibility in selecting their managers. Profits are a byproduct of human capacity. Only a few companies take this responsibility to actualize human capacity as seriously as they should.

LEADERSHIP AND PERSONAL GROWTH

What do we mean by personal growth, particularly as it pertains to managers? On one level, it means developing professional capacities in the basic operations of business—selling, accounting, engineering, manufacturing, etc. These capabilities enable us to be competent but not necessarily generative. To be generative, helping others to become all they are capable of being requires that we ourselves make an inner journey toward higher virtue and advanced maturity.

Each of us is the sum total of every past intention, thought, or action. Attention to our personal growth is simply striving to take the high road in all these venues, whether or not someone else is watching. This kind of growth is driven by a disciplined will, maturity, and love (altruism).

Fidelity to truth is also central to personal growth. Some leaders lie. But more engage in exercises to manipulate other people by spinning information. They exaggerate what makes their point while underplaying or omitting what threatens them or does not support their position. Who loses the most in these spin exercises, the transmitter or the receiver? The receiver, at worst, may get fooled and lose a few pounds of wasted effort. But usually his highly developed HMD protects him. The transmitter, on the other hand, loses the capacity to recognize truth from others because he sees and receives information from others through a lens distorted by his own infidelity to the truth. The transmitter also diminishes his reputation. The prevalence of spin in this country is directly related to the shortage of generative leaders and, because of this shortage, the even larger shortage of trusting followers.

Never confuse credentials for deep growth. Credentials certify professional preparation, not the character required for generative leadership.

Talented leaders usually rise quickly through the socioeconomic echelons. The great ones stay in touch with their roots. That is the key to remaining grounded while at the same time operating at high altitudes. It is important for executives who move to higher responsibilities to be able to see the world from the levels they used to occupy as well as from the commanding heights.

THERE IS NO SHORTCUT

Regardless of your perch in a corporation, leading a change in culture from command-and-control to a governance driven by living up to values, nourishing healthy aspirations, and becoming a learning community is a formidable undertaking. This is true whether you are the CEO of a complex corporation with a hundred thousand employees, the manager of a relatively small self-standing division within a large corporation with a hundred people on the staff, or the small business owner with ten employees. It is an ongoing lifetime's work, for with each step forward, there are new obstacles to overcome and risks to be taken. And as your organization approaches each new plateau, a new mountain will emerge before you have an opportunity to relax and enjoy the perch you have just reached.

How long is a lifetime's work? It took Jack Adam, my predecessor as CEO at Hanover, and me six years to see the linkage between changes in governance and improved economic performance, and twelve years to build a mature values-based, vision-driven culture. By mature culture, I mean a culture in which our experiments in theories of corporate governance were consistently producing superior financial results and widely recognizable individual growth through a process that we knew how to replicate. The substance and flavor of the culture existed in practically every corner of the company.

Why does cultural transformation take so long? Because management has to change some of its long-held mental models (paradigms) and replace long-standing habits. People quickly grasp the intellectual dimension of these ideas, and the overwhelming majority, in my experience, conceptually agrees with them. But internalizing the ideas by moving them from the mind to the heart and stomach, where they are translated into practice, takes quite a bit longer. It requires more than a lesson. There needs to be debate and discussion followed by application of the concepts to authentic situations. Embedding philosophy in an organization requires you to build on small successes, following them with larger ones, while management lives up to the philosophy in times of crisis as well as in good times. In other words, people must see that the new culture works better than the culture being phased out, and must see their managers "walk the talk." While this progress is taking place, there will be alternating periods of skepticism and enthusiasm, of doubt and confidence. All this takes time—although knowing what we know today, and considering the current widespread managerial interest in improving culture, I estimate that the time it took us to transform our culture could be halved. But being on the right track with sound principals and philosophy works better than applying a series of quick fixes that treat symptoms at the surface.

IX.
A PRACTICAL
UNDERSTANDING OF LOVE

I f we are to have a values-based environment in our commercial endeavors, we must have values-based relationships, particularly between individuals at different echelons. We can envision the nature of such relationships as rungs upon a moral ladder.

STEP 1: THE EMPLOYEE AS BUSINESS SERVANT

On the bottom rung of the moral ladder, the employee is treated like a business servant. The manager thinks, "She works for me, therefore her job is to do what I tell her, to please me, and to make me look good. I expect compliance with my directions, and for that I pay the market's wage for a day's work. I parcel out information on a need-to-know basis, for workers, after all, are merely hired hands."

While it is never expressed in such blunt terms, on the business servant rung, a worker is viewed solely as an instrument of production. People working on construction crews can find themselves in this position. So can managers at all echelons in the hierarchy, although white-collar managers usually get a sugar-coated version of the treatment. The boss's behavior is not illegal, nor does it constitute a specific immoral action. The sum total of the relationship, however, discourages the employee from taking on more responsibility, or from experiencing meaning in work, or from using work as a path to happiness. This business servant rung engages only the body, part of the mind, and practically none of the spirit. It is legal

103

and very common, but dispiriting; and, most unfortunately, it is wasteful of human potential.

STEP 2: THE HUMAN RESOURCE PRACTITIONER

The middle rung on our moral ladder belongs to the person whom we shall call the Human Resource Practitioner. This manager says, "I let competent people have wide latitude in performing their responsibilities, keep them informed about the big picture, and reward them through pay and bonuses for results that are better than average." These practices are based on the assumption that good financial performance and customer satisfaction that produces growth are enhanced by attracting and retaining good people—but this rung is still within the command-and-control framework.

Many of our leading companies are on this higher rung of the moral ladder. But it is surprising to see how many workers and managers in these more enlightened companies are still disenchanted. Yes, many workers are afraid of downsizing—but they are also frustrated because their work lacks meaning to them. They note that the command-and-control organization requires that they play political games, and they often lack respect for their senior executives. I am always surprised by the number of operating heads of stellar divisions or subsidiaries of respected corporations who see their own senior executives as the major obstacle to better long-term market and financial performance.

STEP 3: A PRACTICAL UNDERSTANDING OF LOVE

I hesitatingly suggest that the third step on our ladder of increasingly higher moral aspirations be based on a practical understanding of love. Why am I hesitant to suggest this? Because in our Western world, the word "love" has deep connotations we do not normally associate with business—romance, for example, or that special feeling among family members or close friends. But I am not talking about these kinds of relationships. By "love" I mean a predisposition toward helping another person to become complete. This is our primary responsibility to everyone within our purview.

If we believe our businesses will benefit financially if our people enlist their spirit, creativity, and ingenuity in their occupations, shouldn't we then have an intense interest in their deeper happiness? I am not suggesting we should pass out stars to employees or give them other superficial kinds of recognition that have a temporary effect on the spirit. Instead, I am talking about helping them develop to their fullest potential.

What changes in the formation of managers are needed to take the value of love as a concept and put it into practice?

First, we need to understand what love is. Love is not limited to romance, family, and friends but extends to every human endeavor, including the conduct of commerce. Aside from its romantic dimension, love is not something that suddenly strikes us—it is an act of the will.

By "an act of will," I mean that you do not have to like someone to love him or her. Love is an intentional predisposition toward another person. This predisposition can be developed by repetitive effort in the same way we master physical and mental skills. The central question to ask yourself in putting love into practice in the work place is, "What can I do to help Joe, or Mary, or ten thousand employees complete themselves more fully as human beings? How can I help them grow?"

LOVE AND GROWTH

What can we do to manifest love in a practical way on the job? Respect each person. Nurture a predisposition within yourself to help people become ten percent more than they are today. Take the time needed to understand them. Take a reading on the current reality of where they are today. Think about building on their strengths and shoring up their shortcomings. Recognize their on-the-job accomplishments, and honestly but compassionately critique what they can do better. When you assign responsibilities, explain the context of the issues and your aspirations for the operations they are engaged in. Then be interested, but don't micromanage. It's simple and basic—except for developing the predisposition to love in the first place.

While the practice of love is "simple," it is important to beware of simple formulas. I have met many managers who have had significant formative experiences but went away with an incomplete message. For example, a manager may have experienced a leap of personal growth under the stretching conditions of a "no excuse" edict and have gone away with the lesson that people need to be put to the test, rather than the lesson that people need to be understood on their own terms. A mentor's guidance should depend not on formulas or slogans, but on the growth needs of the particular person.

When practicing love by helping another person grow, it is important not to play God. No one can see, with certainty, inside another person. You can know how another's behavior affects you. That is certainly discussable. But that does not get at the underlying cause, which is usually a mental model, attitude, or value that needs adjustment.

In the course of my own life, I have received immense help from mentors who brought up possible dispositions that were impeding my growth. They held up the possibility, acknowledging that the matter was intuitive—that is, not based on data from which they could draw conclusions with certitude. In this sense, they were taking the risk of saying something that could not easily be rationally defended. And they were doing this, as a gift of love, for me. I always knew instantly whether the suggested possibility was on target or irrelevant. On balance, my mentors were more often right than wrong. Today, I deeply appreciate their acts of love toward me. It entailed a lot of work and courage on their part to address my shortcomings—it would have been easier just to let them slide by.

The larger payoff from devoting attention to the personal growth of your employees is the phenomenon of turning satisfactory performers into high performers. Love lubricates the execution of business strategies by raising people's sights, increasing their capacity to trust (thereby reducing fear), and nurturing a general atmosphere of altruism.

This atmosphere of altruism is another way to understand love, for love is not only an act of will, it is also an energy. The psychic fuels that drive corporate performance are fear, greed, applause, pursuit of moral excellence, and love. No company is driven purely by just one fuel—all use a mixture. Compose your own formula, but consider the staying power and unintended consequences of each:

+ *Fear* and *applause* are external forms of motivation. They leave us dependent on an outsider for our energy.
+ *Greed* is addictive and never leaves a sense of enduring fulfillment.
+ *The pursuit of moral excellence* and *love* are internal drivers—under our own control—and are renewable forms of energy, free of unintended negative consequences.

THE PRACTICE OF LOVE IN BUSINESS

Practicing the value of love in business is not a soft undertaking, nor is it without tension. Genuine love goes hand in hand with the pursuit of excellence and high standards. A leader must love both individual people and the enterprise, with its multitude of stakeholders.

I have met leaders who failed because they loved mankind and hated individual people. Others failed because they loved people, and their organizations were incompetent. It is a myth that the practice of love in business comes at the expense of profitability. Sometimes, in the name of compassion, managers fail to address performance issues, and the common good suffers. But this is pseudo love, not the love I am talking about. Just as in parenting, the practice of love requires setting standards as well as accepting individuals on their own terms.

The loving manager is always faced with the pressure of achieving the business imperative while at the same time making decisions for the common good of the organization and of the individuals involved. There are no formulaic answers—but a working knowledge of the age-old values of truth (openness) and justice (merit) are good navigation points to guide the practice of love in business. If a loving manager is quick and tough in addressing issues when they originally surface, most damaging organizational issues can be kept at a minimal level.

Encouragement as an Act of Love

Overconfidence breeds mistakes that lead to setbacks in life. This kind of error is usually visible, the penalty hits home, and the event is stored in our memory for future learning. But underconfidence, I am convinced, breeds far more underrealization of our innate potential than does overconfidence. Further, the missed opportunities are often not reflected upon or stored in our memory, and thus are lost as learning events.

On numerous occasions, a mentor has been invaluable in counseling me, by encouragement, to take steps that I was hesitant to take without the influence of external support. For example, in 1982, Peter Senge invited me to join a group of CEOs to form The New Styles Management Group at MIT's Sloan School of Management. I was hesitant to say yes, partly because I was concerned about my ability to keep up with such a distinguished group of business leaders, and partly because I was concentrated on my single-minded commitment to Hanover's transformation. I talked it over with my wife, Kay, who strongly encouraged me to join up. Her encouragement was an act of love. For me it was the crossing of a threshold to a learning agenda that took me beyond anything that I could have imagined at the time.

It seems to me that traditional bosses are quite conscientious about talking to their people about shortcomings in their performance. Only a few, the inspirational ones, reflect on their people's full utilization of their talent in relation to their work, and encourage them to stretch to their full potential so as to further complete themselves.

CRITICISM AS AN ACT OF LOVE

Pierre Teilhard de Chardin said that "an eye can see everything but itself." If that is true, and I don't see any way of arguing with Teilhard's statement, then we must all depend on others to help us see and develop ourselves. In turn, others depend upon us to see and develop themselves. Thus, occasions arise when criticism is an act of love.

But not all criticism is an act of love. Criticism that vents one's frustrations or is intended to put someone down is egocentric and most often destructive. Criticism that is purely intended to help others complete themselves is an act of love and is constructive. It is also hard work. To criticize another with love requires observable data—in other words, you must observe situations involving the other person in which his or her behavior is an impediment to personal development, and you must have a theory as to why. Bringing together observable data and theory is important. Further, the one making the criticism must have the competence, through experience and maturity, to coach and the credibility to be believed. Spouses, parents, and bosses are the people in the best positions to have the observable data. That is why they can have such powerful influences on human development.

In the early seventies, I joined Hanover as head of marketing operations. In those days, the company was rampant with politics. One of its operating principles was "Please the Boss." Since I was the boss, I thought that would not be a problem. Wrong. For example, the first time Frank, one of our sales managers, came to see me to recommend annual salary adjustments for one of his marketing reps, I suddenly realized that he was in the process of feeling me out rather than coming up with his own best thinking. I did not like the drift of the conversation, so I called time-out and reset a meeting for the next day.

With time to reflect, I realized that Frank had been brought up in a political management environment where disagreement with the boss could have negative consequences. There was also a discrepancy between the budgeted average merit increase and the appropriate reward for superior performance. Beyond that, I knew Frank was a clear thinker and possessed a deep sense of fairness. At the meeting the next day, I called him to task for taking me through a feeling-out process rather than letting me have the benefit of his best thinking, including specific recommendations. By handling the matter in a feeling-out mode, he had deprived me of his best thinking and had not done justice to the marketing rep, who deserved the best evaluation we could make. Further, Frank was stunting the development of his own decision-making capacities by engaging in the lame game of politics. When we ended "Please the Boss" politics, Frank became an outstanding marketing vice president.

These and other experiences have taught me that while criticism born out of anger and frustration is usually destructive, criticism born out of love is usually productive—if not immediately, then after reflection. Love and truth go hand in hand. Many of the impediments to growth, such as poor attitudes, undeveloped mental models, hurtful habits, and wrong priorities, are difficult to talk about. It is a favor, sometimes unwanted, to open up this kind of conversation with a manager stumbling in his or her job. It is especially hard when the manager is not stumbling now, but is on track to stumble later. Quite often, to help others grow requires inflicting short-term hurt—for example, telling them what they would rather not hear. Delivering or receiving this kind of message is not fun. But when it is done for the purpose of growth and not to hurt, it is a loving act. When it is genuine, it is more often appreciated than not, even when it hurts.

When you devote deep thought to someone's performance, give a similar amount of thought to both used and underused capacities. If you reflect on these capacities in the context of the whole person, while holding a predisposition to help him or her, whatever the outcome, the person will generally see through the pain and form a special appreciation of your interest. These are moments when love is powerful.

People can be fired with love. The decision to fire a manager ought to be taken only after serious effort has been made to coach him or her toward satisfactory performance. If, after coaching, the manager continues to fail to meet standards, the leader's first responsibility is to the health of the enterprise. There should be a best effort to provide an economic bridge to cover the normal time it takes to find another job. The individual should also receive the benefit of advice that will help him or her succeed elsewhere, and your support in moving on in his or her career.

Companies frequently neglect to weed their gardens. Over time, they accumulate a number of managers who let down other elements of the organization. Many companies cannot fire one, two, or three people, but they know how to downsize three thousand. That is not love, that is negligence. Leaders must love their people and their enterprise while having the courage to consistently maintain high standards of performance.

SHARING THE CONTEXT BEHIND ISSUES

My first years in management were during the early sixties, when the dominant organization in the field of management was the American Management Association. It taught that the definition of management was planning, organizing, and controlling. Yet the best managers I was meeting on the job were not planners, organizers, or controllers, but great teachers. What did they teach? The context of the situation at hand, so that I could fully use my thinking apparatus to get the job done, even when circumstances were changing as the job was underway.

The business world is full of people frustrated and disenchanted by micromanagers who cannot trust the people who work for them.

Managers who play their cards close to their vests seldom inspire others. Managers who lay all the cards on the table, which usually means sharing the context of an issue, seem to bring out the best in their people. At the same time, they raise productivity in its broadest sense. Sharing context helps people complete themselves. It is an act of love.

SERVING AS A SOUNDING BOARD TO LIFT THE FOG

When you are in the middle of the action, whether it involves upgrading a culture or improving strategy, there is a lot of fog. Only years later, when you tell it as an old story, does everything become crystal clear. On numerous occasions in my career, the opportunity to talk through issues with a trusted mentor has been invaluable in lifting the fog from complex issues. I can take interconnected and complex ideas only so far by myself. Then I need a listener. Sometimes just the opportunity to talk complex issues through with someone brings the clarity. At other times, my partner adds a key insight or just affirms enough to overcome my doubts. No matter which, having a sounding board helps me grow toward completeness. And I equally value the occasions when I have been able to help others just by listening to their thoughts about which we share a common passion.

GENERATIVE LEADERSHIP

Helping others grow is a fundamental attribute of generative leaders—it is the practice of love. The similarities between generative leadership and good parenting are striking—maybe you cannot do either unless you can do both. But whether or not managers are parents, they all have a responsibility to encourage human growth.

There are three central dimensions in the generation of human growth. First, we must pay never-ending attention to our own growth, including the capacity to practice love. Second, we must devote ourselves to paying similar attention to the growth of those people who report directly to us. Third, we must shape the cultural architecture of our area of responsibility: to respect each individual and the dignity of all work, to value learning and maturing, and to promote the pursuit of excellence.

Leaders are the primary architects of culture. They have two main tools for culture building: their theories and their actions. Their theories should be congruent with the evolving nature of humans, and their actions should be congruent with their theories. The latter congruency spells integrity. The former constitutes competency.

I would rather put in a job a person whose leadership capacities are at eight on their way to nine, than a person whose capacities were at ten and are on their way to nine. Why? Because the process of growth is contagious. If the boss is growing, it is more likely that the people will too. Unfortunately, the reverse is also true.

All leaders leave a wake that impacts the people in their domain. Weak leaders leave little impact in their wake. Degenerative leaders create cultures that pull people down so that they become less and less of what they are capable of becoming. But generative leaders leave a wake that uplifts people and inspires them to grow and achieve the highest potential of which they are capable.

X.
MATURITY

When we talk about expressing love by helping someone grow, what kind of growth are we talking about? In a business setting at the higher levels, most likely it is maturity. How does maturity relate to leadership effectiveness? Let's use the back door to get to this question: Why do people flunk out of senior management positions? Is it because they lack ambition, or lack the needed intelligence, or fail to work hard? Seldom in my thirty-five years of experience have I found these to be the causes of failure. Instead, it is generally because they fail to energize their people or to get interdependent departments to cooperate around an economic purpose. We superficially name this kind of failure a "personality issue" or a problem with "fit." But, at a deep structural level, the failure is caused by a lack of size—the person is not "big" enough for the job. By size I mean the stage of advancement of the manager's maturity in relation to the other people involved and the complexity of the issues. In leadership, truthfulness, trustworthiness, wisdom, and altruism constitute maturity. These are qualities driven by love, the gift of helping others grow.

PATHS TO MATURITY

There are three main paths to maturity. The first is the lonely inner journey of shaping core beliefs and making our choices congruent with our beliefs. The second is what we do. And the third is what we undergo. Don't underestimate the possibilities of the latter. Enormous growth emerges from adversity when we maintain an appropriate disposition. I know of instances where suffering an egocentric boss, a bad marriage, or even prison resulted in extraordinary personal growth.

FIGURE 4. PATHS TO MATURITY

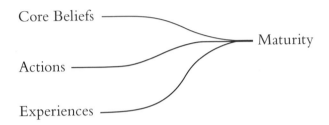

The barriers to maturity are fear, anger, and selfish desire. These same barriers cloud judgment.

EMOTIONAL DEVELOPMENT

Individual development is a complex process involving the total person—physical, intellectual, and emotional. Yet today most of our energy seems to be focused on the first two. All about us is evidence of our preoccupation with physical development. Fitness and wellness are not just trends; they are also big business. On the streets of any city or town in America, in magazines and books, in fitness centers and sporting goods shops all across the nation, we see evidence of our national passion for physical development.

We also see a great deal of concern for intellectual development, a concern visible not only in traditional educational institutions, but also in the growing adult education movement in colleges, seminars, and corporate training programs.

But whatever the reasons, we do not pursue full emotional development with the same intensity with which we pursue physical and intellectual development. This is all the more unfortunate since full emotional development offers the greatest degree of leverage in attaining our full potential.

When we talk about full emotional development, we are talking about the fullness of maturity, much as wisdom is the fullness of knowledge. For want of a more precise term, I call that state "advanced maturity." It presupposes a basic level of maturity, much as wisdom requires a certain degree of knowledge; yet in many ways it goes beyond conventional notions of maturity. Because attaining this state of advanced maturity is so essential to our success and happiness as human beings, I wish I knew an easy way to attain it. But there is no magic formula that guarantees us this type of maturity if only we will spend a certain number of minutes a day doing specific exercises. In fact, I would be highly suspicious of any formula that makes such promises. Acquiring advanced maturity is a process, an adventure, a lifetime journey. Different travelers may progress at different rates, but there are no shortcuts.

The best guideposts for this journey toward advanced maturity are the characteristics that we see in highly mature people.

CHARACTERISTICS OF MATURE LEADERS

1) Strong Convictions

One of the most striking characteristics of highly mature people is the degree to which they are guided by strong beliefs and values. They seem to go through a process of opening themselves to ideas, considering them, testing them, and finally deciding whether they want to internalize them and make them a part of their inner core of beliefs and values. These strong convictions give them a sense of direction, enabling them to achieve more than the average person in our society does.

The result is a well-developed ability to distinguish that which is enduring from that which is passing. Those who possess this ability are less susceptible to media hype or passing fads than the rest of the population. Though they may at times appear to move slowly, their inner beliefs give them a discernible sense of direction.

In his books on excellence and self-renewal, John Gardner tells us that a society that does not believe in anything will never attain excellence. This is as true of you and me as individuals as it is of organizations, the United States, or the free world. Strong beliefs and values are at the root of all achievement.

2) Commitments

Highly mature people lead committed lives. Their commitments flow from their beliefs about significant matters: the importance of the family, the way society should work, the way organizations should function. More than most people, they are able to maintain priorities among multiple commitments.

Genuine commitment is always to something larger than ourselves. We have all observed the person whose attitude proclaims: "I'm committed to getting as much out of this for myself as I possibly can." Such an attitude is actually a parody of commitment. And though it may seem to bring some short-term gains, in the long run it often fails to live up to its promises. Certainly, it is powerless to produce genuine happiness because true happiness comes to us as a byproduct. We obtain it not by seeking it for itself, but through our commitments to people and to things other than ourselves. If happiness through commitment and convictions is such an open secret, why don't more people experience it? Why aren't we a happier society?

I believe that the biggest obstacle to commitment is not laziness, indifference, or even selfishness, but rather a fear of being vulnerable. Commitment carries certain risks. It brings with it the possibility of failure. To protect themselves, many people refuse to be vulnerable. "After all," they say, "what if it doesn't work out?" Or "I'll try it out and see how it goes." Ironically, such attitudes become self-fulfilling prophecies. Their possessors never realize—or realize only belatedly—that they have protected themselves not only from pain and failure but also from some of life's greatest joys. The opposite is also true. Those who give themselves completely seem to find what they are seeking.

The achievement of anything worthwhile, including happiness, requires risk. This is true in our personal lives, in our marriages, in our relationships, and in our careers. A low-risk life will not produce high-level happiness.

3) Openness

Highly mature people are open. They admit their limitations and reveal their feelings and concerns. They don't feel they have to know everything. And they are good listeners.

Sometimes we meet people who have an inflated sense of their own importance. In my early days in business, I was impressed by the number of highly successful executives who were disarmingly open, who listened, asked questions, encouraged others, and even admitted their own limitations. Their openness presented a sharp contrast to other, more pompous managers, who were primarily concerned with the image they were projecting, and who played their cards close to their vests.

4) Free Will

Highly mature people have an inner strength that comes from exercising their free will. All of us started our lives with wills that were free but which, little by little, became enslaved. Part of that enslavement occurred through the circumstances of our upbringing. Another part of it resulted from choices we made along the way. There are different kinds and degrees of enslavement. Individuals with addictions experience one kind; those who are driven mainly by insular self-interest experience another. Yet all of us, to one degree or another, find that we no longer possess the freedom to which we were born.

The highest exercise of our free will is to maintain harmony between what we believe and what we do. Psychologists tell us that we have an intangible core in our deepest being that is composed of our values, our beliefs, and our convictions. We experience feelings of wholeness and inner harmony when our actions are in alignment with this core. Conversely, we are torn apart when our actions are in conflict with our core beliefs and values.

This lack of alignment shows up in those who are drifting as well as in those who are obviously experiencing conflict. "I've got to get my act together" reveals a person who is "out of sync" as much as does the conflict of the person who is doing things he or she does not believe in.

We need to experience alignment not only within ourselves, but also between ourselves and the organization for which we work. This doesn't mean that we can expect satisfaction from every task every day. Every job contains some drudgery. Our personal alignment is not threatened when our job requires us to do things we don't like to do, but only when it demands that we do things we don't believe in. Companies should not ask their employees to do anything that violates their personal convictions or which interferes with their inner alignment.

5) Deferred Gratification

Highly mature people make choices that defer gratification. By choosing future rewards over those within easy reach, they free themselves from the tyranny of the short term and gain greater control over their destinies.

We live in a society that encourages us to seek instant gratification. If we have a headache, we take a pill. If we are cold, we turn up the thermostat. If we are bored, we flip on the television. The same desire for instant results also afflicts corporations. An emphasis on current results can replace the long-term view. We saw this instant gratification syndrome at work in the automobile industry in the late 1970s. While the Japanese were installing the latest equipment in their plants, American automobile manufacturers were sacrificing reinvestment on the altar of higher earnings.

6) Accurate Maps

Highly mature people possess accurate maps of reality. It is not so much that mature individuals have better information than everyone else, but rather that they have the knack of putting the same information into better perspective. This is because their lenses are less distorted by the self-delusions that result from clinging to immature styles of adjustment. The immature pay a high price for choosing the safe rut over what is sometimes a scary path of self-examination.

7) Moral Courage

Highly mature people possess moral courage. They have the ability to make tough or unpopular decisions, the strength to tell people what they don't want to hear, and the willingness to ask people to do what they would rather not do.

Moral courage is the process we go through every time we risk a penalty in order to achieve a worthwhile goal. It is a necessary way to become both liberated and mature. For each of us, the ultimate question is this: From the person I now am, how do I become everything I am capable of being? Most of us can recall a time when we took a risk and found ourselves liberated. Very likely, we also remember another occasion when we settled for what seemed to be the safe route and felt trapped or unsatisfied. Being willing to take risks doesn't mean becoming a daredevil or an adventurer. It doesn't mean turning decision making into a crapshoot. To me, it means taking calculated risks, which is exactly the opposite of making rash or impulsive decisions. We take a calculated risk every time we face an issue, do our homework, test the idea in discussions, conclude that there are significant benefits at stake, decide that what we are seeking to achieve is consistent with our own values and best judgment, and then act on our decision.

Think, for example, about the decision to marry a particular person. Although momentous decisions usually take place in the deepest recesses of our hearts, it is usually the externals that get the most attention: choosing the site for the reception, selecting the band, deciding on the color of the bridesmaids' dresses. There is a tendency to pour a great deal of energy into the public display, often to the detriment of the private moments. But that's getting it backwards. It is the private moments of decision making and risk taking that determine future happiness—while few wedding ceremonies can be called unsuccessful, many marriages fail.

It takes moral courage to make the right choice between hard and easy, desirable and undesirable, playing safe and being vulnerable. All of us regularly face some of the following choices in our personal lives and at work:

+ A choice between facing or avoiding a new and perhaps intimidating challenge.
+ A choice between dealing with or avoiding conflict.
+ A choice between speaking up for the minority view or going with the tide of the majority.
+ A choice between risking rejection or taking what appears to be a safer course.

THE LADDER OF MATURATION

Advancing our maturity, especially our capacity to take risks, is a little like climbing a ladder. The higher we climb, the more skill, courage, and maturity we gain. When we are on the bottom rung, the steps halfway up seem frightening. Yet each time we climb a step higher, we acquire the ability to master all the risks at that level. By the time we measure up to the risks at the higher steps, the risks at the lower rungs, which once appeared so difficult, suddenly appear manageable.

Infancy—obviously, is the lowest rung—the first phase and most immature stage. Self-centeredness reigns supreme. We have no sense of others' needs or of fitting in—we simply want what we want when we want it, and if it is not forthcoming, we bawl our heads off. This kind of behavior is understandable because we are fully dependent on others for our every need.

Then *adolescence* arrives. The tension between self-centeredness and other-centeredness is heightened. On one hand, society imposes benchmarks for us to get ahead. Schools have precise marking systems to presumably measure certain kinds of learning, diplomas are required to move ahead to better opportunities, and peer pressure is fierce. On the other hand, within each of us, our own unique personality is beginning to take a more distinct shape. It is a time of rebelling against the imposed strictures. Up to a point, this rebellion is normal and healthy at this age. Most of us during this time are primarily outer-directed rather than reflective—and some of us never leave this stage.

Adulthood One follows, the time for getting established in life. We pick a career, obtain a position, choose a mate, form aspirations, create a philosophy of life, and make decisions that impact our future station in life. Our self-centeredness is becoming more balanced with other-centeredness. It is an energetic but competitive time. Many of us plateau in this phase, with the downside that life loses its zest and meaning, and we lose our sense of fulfillment. The upside is that it is less taxing to level off.

For those who keep climbing, *Adulthood Two* follows. It is a time of consolidating and building upon the gains of the previous phase. This

FIGURE 5. THE LADDER OF MATURATION

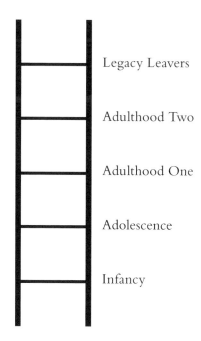

Legacy Leavers

Adulthood Two

Adulthood One

Adolescence

Infancy

stage might entail taking on more responsibility for others at work, seeing the larger picture, acquiring more turf and a higher title, moving to a larger home in a better neighborhood, and gaining professional recognition. At the same time, we become more inner-directed. Only a small percentage of gifted people achieve the Adulthood Two phase. This phase is comfortable, but dangerous. If we get stuck in it, the temptation toward materialism is high. So again we face a choice: level off or keep climbing. Toward what?

The highest stage I have identified we could call *Legacy Leavers*. They move on from a major focus on consolidating their gains to taking responsibility for the quality of the enterprise they will leave to coming generations. They truly take responsibility for the future. They look deep within themselves and their organizations while reaching out to the larger world. They outgrow the driving compulsions to acquire and impress, replacing them with genuine altruism. They understand what is and envision what ought to be. They possess a healthy self-centeredness, but it is in service to other-centeredness.

This journey from adolescence and its normal self-centeredness to leaving a legacy encompasses developing a metaphysical belief system and achieving an advanced stage of psychological maturity. I believe this journey is at the heart of business transformation. It is a journey full of risks and rewards. This quality of maturity has to be widely spread throughout the organization for renewal to be a way of corporate life. Once achieved, it is an enduring competitive advantage.

THE INFLUENCE OF ENVIRONMENT ON MATURITY

No one can make me mature. Only I can do that for myself. Nevertheless, environment has a powerful influence on our growth and maturation. Fishermen know this. Fish thrive in unpolluted water. If their habitat is polluted, their population shrinks, they decrease in size, and they lose their vitality. In a few years, they may completely disappear. Environment—whether we call it "society" or "corporate culture"—has the same effect on the physical and emotional development of the human species.

What kind of environment nourishes high maturity and the risk-taking it requires?

"If you want people to take risks," the common wisdom goes, "you have to be willing to accept failure." Like so many slogans, this one is partly true. After all, few people will take chances if failure is automatically greeted with harsh penalties. However, think about this for a moment: If all the penalties were removed, wouldn't the risk be eliminated, too? The built-in penalties are what make risk risky. Taking growth-producing risks requires courage. But the rewards are a feeling of having measured up and the conviction that you can respond to whatever challenges come your way.

Successful organizations encourage their people to stretch and take risks despite the possibility that they will occasionally make mistakes or fail. They know it is better for a person to make ten decisions and be right seven times than to take only one chance, even if that one turns out to be right. But while successful organizations encourage risk-taking, they cannot tolerate unlimited mistakes or eliminate all the penalties. The presence of risk, with all its dangers, encourages people to stretch and leads to high performance. The absence of risk lulls people into complacency, which leads to mediocrity or even failure.

Environments that nourish risk-taking and encourage personal maturity do not eliminate penalties. Rather, they develop governing ideas that are congruent with the most deeply held principles of their people. When the principles of our company are the same as our own, we are able to take risks for what we believe in and are committed to, even though we are aware of the potential penalties for failure.

WHY ARE YOU IN BUSINESS?

Transforming a corporation is a formidable task because so much has to change in individuals and in the organization. Usually when we look at organizations, we focus our attention on "what we do around here." What we do around here—what every business does—is operate a number of financial, production, and selling systems that produce goods and services in order to make money. These physical systems—balance sheets, income statements, manufacturing formulas, marketing strategies, and so forth—are critically important. But changing these physical systems will not result in organizational transformation.

There is another level of organizational activity, described by "how we do things around here." This is organizational culture, the manifestation of our social beliefs and behavioral norms, how we work with each other and our customers. Changing "how we do things around here" by imposing different social norms is important. But it will not create transformation either.

There is yet another, deeper level: "Why we do what we do around here." This is the deepest structural level of organizational life. It is about purpose, intention, and values. It goes beyond the previously mentioned physical and cultural systems. Philosophers call this kind of thought "a metaphysical belief system." Organizational transformation happens at this deepest level. An ennobling metaphysical belief system around purpose, intention, and values—when put into practice—fuels the human attributes of commitment, creativity, and cooperation required to achieve high-performance business results. Change the why and the how and the what will follow.

Lots of people get these levels confused. When asked, "Why are you in business?" they say, "To make money." That is what businesses do—not why they do it. I was in the insurance business: What we did was sell insurance policies that transferred the risk of loss from the individual to the company; why we did it had to do with our beliefs about human purpose, corporate purpose, human nature, responsibility to our customers, and the role of work in each person's life. In other words, why we did what we did had to do with our metaphysical belief system.

If you are a business leader who wishes to create a transformational organization, you have to have a metaphysical belief system.

Most leaders are unprepared for this challenge because most leaders have risen to positions of responsibility by mastering physical systems. They are superb accountants and engineers and marketers; they are people with savvy and social skills and abundant common sense. But leading an organization—especially a transformational organization—requires more. Not only must you develop a metaphysical belief system, but also, like an orchestra conductor, you must make sure that all the company systems—metaphysical, cultural, and physical—work together harmoniously. As you move your organization forward, you have to make sure that the material and cultural systems—the what and how of your business—don't overwhelm the why. The most important job for a leader, whether you are the CEO, a manager, or a supervisor, is to maintain the harmony among the interconnected belief systems. Focus on metaphysical beliefs and let the material and cultural systems serve these ideas—but make sure the financial and measurement systems that govern your business activities function at the highest possible level.

PURPOSE AND VALUES

Spreading and internalizing beliefs about purpose and values in a culture that honors free choice is the essence of transformation. But unless the leadership community shares a belief system, transformation will not endure over generations of management. Often, a charismatic leader with loyal followers can achieve high performance and the appearance of transformation for a while; but when the leader leaves, the apparent transformation folds. And be mindful: for ideas about purpose and values to take hold in an authentic manner, people must voluntarily accept them. Often managers tend to force the acceptance of their ideas on subordinates through subtle tricks of coercion, rather than letting the attractiveness of noble purpose, sound values, and pure intention bring their people to voluntary commitment. While being patient, respect your people and trust that they will respond to purpose and values that lead to the high road.

For competitive advantage you don't need 100 percent followership. You just need more than your competitors. Don't let frustration with the few water down your enthusiasm for nurturing your
organization's core philosophy.

Moving Up the Values Food Chain

Two forces are powerful enough to impel organizational change at
this deepest level. The first and easiest to understand comes from outside the organization. Something happens that changes the ground
rules of the business. The government passes a law, for example, or a
technological innovation renders a particular business or even an industry obsolete. When these environmental changes are big enough,
the organization must completely reinvent itself to survive. The what,
the how, and, most importantly, the why are up for grabs.

The second force comes from inside the organization. It is an or-
ganization-wide commitment to moving up the values food chain.
Some people think of values as either/or propositions—honesty vs.
dishonesty, or responsibility vs. irresponsibility. These are values at the
most basic level. Once you commit to a value like honesty, for example, you have before you a spectrum of possible behavior. At one end
of the spectrum, honesty could mean simply avoiding lies; at the other
end of the spectrum is full and forthright disclosure of everything
about the subject, with absolutely no intent to manipulate. There is a
world of difference between the two. When an organization commits
to moving up the values food chain, everything changes.

A Bump on the Head

We don't move up the values food chain easily. It happens to me
by bumping my head in frustration until I get to the point where I
think, "Maybe I ought to try to change." Then I try to change. It
never works perfectly, and it never works quickly. I have to go
through a period of struggle until I internalize the value. Once I do

change, I want my colleagues to change, too. So I call them and tell them all about it. I expect them to change in five minutes—never mind that it took me six months or six years. Then I get angry when it takes them as long as it took me.

If I am all stirred up with anger or fear, or if I am blinded by desire, my ability to lead transformation is diminished. But if I go through the internal process of mastering my desires and being peaceful, the inner serenity that results lifts the fog. It is part of rising above the ordinary—which is essential in transformation.

I point all this out because when we talk about transformation, we are talking about doing it throughout the organization. It is a time-consuming process. And it is a personal process because to transform an organization, you first have to transform yourself.

INTENTION, MATURITY, AND LOVE

Adam Kahane, my partner at Generon Consulting, once told me about a workshop he did for the bishops in the Episcopal synod in South Africa. At the beginning of the workshop, the bishops discussed their intent. "What we intend," they said, "is to listen to the sacredness in every person, to listen to every person with the intention of being loving."

Now, this might make sense for a religious group, but what could it possibly have to do with business? I will tell you: everything. It translates into committed workers and leaders who, in turn, raise productivity and improve relationships inside and outside of the corporate family. "Love thy neighbor" has been a precept since the days of Moses—3,400 years ago. If it has lasted that long—113 generations—why shouldn't we apply it in business? Through our work, we have great responsibility for other people. Our decisions influence the lives of the people in our organizations—and the lives of their families. There is no getting away from this. A central part of that responsibility is to love our neighbor—particularly those neighbors in our own "flock."

When it comes to transformation, the maturity of the leadership matters. Usually, the top person in a company has a lot of options. If he doesn't want to, he won't change the company. Then there is the next level of leadership—also extremely influential. These are the people to whom most of the people in the organization report. The whole organization—sometimes tens of thousands of people—looks to those fifteen or so people and says, "Are they going to walk the talk that the CEO espouses? Or are they simply paying lip service to what the leader's talking about?" To lead a transformation, that group of people must outgrow the gain-consolidating phase of life and begin to think of the legacy that they are leaving.

Take a Look Inside

The best place to begin the quest for organizational transformation is by examining what you want to do with the rest of your professional life. When I was in my late thirties, the question I posed to myself was "Do I want to spend the rest of my life adapting to office politics and all the other ecological pollution that infests the typical command-and-control company? Or do I want to devote it to building the kind of company where I would want to start out if I were beginning my career over again?"

Why is this question important? Because there is a lot of perceived personal economic risk entailed in pushing for the transformation of cultures. Perceived risk is based on fear of a negative event in our lives. I use the phrase perceived risk because I believe the estimated risk is usually much greater than the actual risk.

Fear of risk causes tentativeness, which, when excessive, diminishes our effectiveness as leaders. Courage is not the absence of fear. Only mindless people are free of fear. Courage is overcoming fear. How do you overcome fear? By internalizing the conviction that the goals you are accomplishing are worth risking the penalties you face. Sacrifice is made sensible. Put differently, the perseverance, courage, stamina, and determination necessary to overcome the inertia, skepticism, and systemic resistance to cultural transformation are rooted in the leader's beliefs and depth of conviction. The self-discipline to live up to the values and ideas you espouse are likewise anchored in your depth of conviction. It comes back to Gandhi's observation that transformation takes place when you become the change that you wish to see in the world.

CHARACTER AND THE CORPORATION

So, you have decided what you want to do with the remainder of your professional life and where you are headed. What's next? As you already know, there are no formulas. You start the journey, usually in the circumstance in which you find yourself. Don't let yourself get bogged down in minutiae or be deluded that you need to know all the answers before you start. Your responsibility is to know moral principles, human nature, human needs, and human values, and how best to apply this knowledge to ordinary business tasks. You do not need to micromanage each person or situation. Be confident that, over time, high-quality principles will drive out low-quality principles when leaders with integrity, who live by the values they espouse, advocate them.

So, in summary, what are the characteristics of a mature leader?

✦ Being a person who has cultivated a philosophy of life that reaches beyond innate self-centeredness to genuine "other-centeredness." Teilhard de Chardin once wrote "I knew I was maturing when I could read about an event that benefited the common good, but negatively impacted myself, and rejoice."

✦ Being a person who makes and keeps multiple commitments.

✦ Being a person who listens, who is confident, who makes himself or herself vulnerable in conversation in order to learn and to make better decisions.

✦ Being a person who is mindful about exercising his or her will—that is, doing what one should do rather than what one wants to do.

✦ Being a person who can delay gratification and who possesses the capacity to forego today's reward for the kinds of rewards that take time to earn.

✦ Being a person who has the simplicity and purity to understand and see clearly the affairs of business and businesspeople. At the core of this quality is purity of intention combined with the ability to strip complex matters to their essence.

✦ Being a person with the will to overcome fear.

Transformation of an organization, large or small, is a formidable task. In fact, transforming oneself—just one person—is a big job. I believe that to lead deep organizational change, you have to do both at the same time—a stretching task for even the most gifted and energetic managers. Transformation means rising above the ordinary, overcoming the powerful gravitational pull to be part of the crowd—to be just another company in an overpopulated marketplace. At its essence, it entails a complicated process through which an individual decides to substitute the practice of higher values for lesser ones and a more appropriate mental model for a less effective one.

Maturity is a never-ending journey. We can't teach it, but we can help one another along the road. That's what the great leaders do.

Part 4

PUTTING PRINCIPLES INTO PRACTICE

Put simply, by combining good people with a healthy culture, we did what we knew we should be doing better than most of our competitors. It was more virtue than smarts—the good of the whole was put ahead of self-interest.

XI.
PUTTING PRINCIPLES INTO PRACTICE

I offer the ideas in this book with the hope that they will help in the construction of corporate cultures that bring out the best in people, while delivering high customer satisfaction and superior financial performance, without which all "people-building" exercises in a corporate setting are either empty or temporary.

The ideas I have proposed are a significant departure from the ones on which the traditional corporate hierarchical pyramid is based. But the governance of business is a practical matter, and ideas ungrounded in practice, while they may be interesting philosophically, are not really very useful. So that you can judge for yourself the extent to which these ideas might be useful—and how they might be useful—I have included this section on my experience of putting these principles into practice at Hanover. I also think that ideas have more meaning when you understand the circumstances out of which they emerged and who the person espousing them is.

ROOTS

I am a Christian and a capitalist, in that order. The early formative experiences in my life were loving parents, a parochial school education followed by college at a Jesuit University, and two years of service in the U.S. Army as an enlisted man. The Jesuits imbued in me a lifelong appetite to go deeper into the causes of outcomes, while the Army introduced me to a "no-excuse" culture and taught me how to get along with and respect people from every walk of life. Additionally, the experience in the Army gave me a chance to see firsthand how a large organization actually works at the bottom, particularly in relation to human responses and interactions. I learned a lifelong lesson: You can't B.S. the troops.

After completing my Army service, I went to work in the insurance industry. I loved it. The game of business was my calling. It was a field on which I could play out the two driving forces within me—to live my faith (grow spiritually) and to contribute to my fellow human's well-being (grow professionally). I had a vehicle for integrating my Christianity with my occupation, though it was important to keep up the appearance of separation.

I started at the bottom as a clerk in an accounting department. Later, I spent a dozen years at the very top of a major corporation. What I learned at the bottom had a strong influence on what I did at the top. I saw myself more as an architect of culture and strategy than as a commander of a business, though I was always conscious of being in charge.

A STORY ABOUT PERFORMANCE

This story covers a twenty-two-year period, from 1969 to 1991. I was the CEO for twelve years, from 1979 to 1991. Jack Adam, under whom I served as head of marketing for eight years, was my predecessor from 1969 to 1979. Under our stewardship the philosophy of corporate governance described in this book was conceived, tested, implemented, and nourished.

A word about performance: In the insurance industry, companies can achieve high premium growth by lowering their underwriting standards and prices. If they take this route, they will grow like gangbusters for a while, but soon their profitability will sour. They will then usually tighten their selection standards (underwriting) so much that agents will reduce the volume and quality of business with them. This shift in approach to customers is behind the expressions "buyer's market" and "seller's market."

Superior insurance companies are not immune from these cyclical forces, but they can significantly better the industry averages for combined ratios and premium growth in both adverse and prosperous phases of the cycle. When I refer to "bottom-of-the-industry" and "upper-quarter" results, I am referring to our management of these ratios in comparison to industry averages.

Insurance companies also hold a lot of money from which they earn considerable investment income that either augments their earnings or offsets their losses from insurance operations. But the key to superior results and distinctiveness in the insurance business is on the operating side, and that is where ninety-nine percent of our people worked.

THE BUSINESS OF TRANSFORMATION

The difficult issues in a transformation process include devolving power while maintaining discipline; keeping the maturity of managers ahead of the momentum of the company's growth curve; and clearing out the political and bureaucratic currents that misdirect human energy. This chapter attempts to offer practical responses to these difficult issues.

Many people have asked me, "How does a company that has undergone a transformation look? What's different?"

My answer is that ninety-five percent of a transformational change in a business takes place inside people—inside their mental models, dispositions, perspectives, and attitudes. These aren't easily visible to a casual observer. The visible exterior changes are fewer levels of management; less structure; less emphasis on rank, rules, and procedures; and more emphasis on human judgment and shared visions.

What, then, were the interior transformations that went on inside me and others as we guided Hanover Insurance Company from the bottom of the property and casualty insurance industry in 1969 to a position consistently in the upper quarter for the decade of the eighties?

FIRST STAGE: CLIMBING OFF THE BOTTOM

Humans frequently die suddenly. But big institutions usually die slowly from decay, gradually descending down the food chain in the quality of their constituents. For example, the employees they attract are less productive and creative than the ones who built the enterprise, their customers are less discerning, their leaders are more political and bureaucratic, vendors see them as less desirable clients, and the vendors' employees prefer to be assigned to other clients. Depending on the organization's size, the amount of accumulated capital, and the competitive condition of the industry as a whole, this descent down the food chain may take years, or even decades, before it culminates in a death spiral.

Hanover was founded in 1842 and reached its peak around 1948. When Jack Adam began the comeback effort in 1969, we were on the edge of the death spiral, having descended down the food chain for two decades. At the time, we were approaching the company's 127th birthday.

What was it like at the bottom of the food chain? The company had an inferiority complex, which was earned—we were inferior. We didn't admit it, but we felt it. We approached our agents for growth with hat in hand. We felt insecure because we were not bringing to market the products and services that many of our competitors offered.

To fix the organization, we needed talented people, better automation, and education to increase skills. But money was scarce. Vision, aspirations, and imagination were even scarcer. We could not afford consultants, so if we were going to turn the organization around, we had to figure out how, and do it ourselves. Our financial rating was low in an industry where financial strength was critical. Someone once described the insurance industry as "the walking army of the disenchanted." We fit the description. Our nickname in the industry was "The Hangover."

When I reach inside myself to ask how it felt to be at the bottom of the food chain, the response is complex. The word "shame" comes to mind, but it is not entirely accurate. Shame is a feeling that grows out of a failure of personal responsibility. Hanover's condition, at the time, was an institutional failure I was engaged in fixing, not one I had caused. For me, the hard part of being at the bottom was an inner feeling of absence—the absence of the satisfaction, the excitement, the respect that comes with building and being part of an institution that is improving how it serves society. A theologian once told me that he thought the most painful suffering in hell was the absence of the joy and peace of heaven. Maybe the severest pain at the bottom of the food chain is the absence of the inner feeling that comes from contributing to an organization that, in turn, is contributing to a better world.

My experience at the bottom left an indelible imprint on me of what leadership responsibility is all about, and how critical it is for an organization to get better every month in order to avoid "plateauing." Plateauing is an interim step to the onset of decay—and decay inevitably leads to a descent down the food chain. The most fundamental responsibility of a leader, the essence of his or her stewardship, is to keep the constituencies ascending. The kind of ascending I am talking about is the interior growth of the people who make the business work.

How do you get an organization off the bottom? You have to start with a leader, or preferably a small leadership team. These leaders must be believable and competent in their area of professional responsibility, with a competence that is in proportion to the task at hand. John Gardner, the Secretary of Health, Education and Welfare under Lyndon Johnson, once said, "If a society venerates philosophers and denigrates plumbers, neither its pipes or theories will hold water." In business, good philosophy won't overcome technical incompetence.

Next, there must be a story that people can believe and commit to. The story must paint a picture of the "Promised Land" that is both attractive and doable, and it must have an inspirational dimension. It must be more than a projection of numbers and dollars—it has to come from inside the leader. Canned stories come from the memory, but this one must come from the heart. Canned stories don't inspire buy-in. Jack Adam once told me that "One person speaking with conviction is a majority on most committees."

The story I began to tell when we were on the bottom had three parts. I frequently used a flip chart so I could tap into my listeners' minds visually as well as verbally. And I adjusted the length of the story to a minute or two short of my listeners' attention span. My guiding principle was "A star sings one song too few; a has-been sings one song too many."

To make sure the continuity of the story didn't get lost, I used a framework of stair-steps. The bottom step was connecting with our roots. My intention was to honor the past, making the point that we had survived for over a century and a quarter. In any collective activity, we all stand on the shoulders of the generations that precede us. Many managers who take on a turnaround talk as if the world began the day they arrived—thus implicitly condemning the past work of the people they depend on to reverse their descent. This tactic is unlikely to elicit support.

My second step on the staircase was current reality, the sea-worthiness of our ship and how we compared to our competitors in the industry. I was as candid as I knew how to be. Most declining companies are focused inward and find themselves comparing the inept performance of one department against another department's inadequacies. I wanted us to begin focusing on the standards of the competitive marketplace.

The top step was what ought to be—my dream for the organization. I told them that I wanted Hanover to be unquestionably superior. Even though I could not define what I meant by this phrase, I knew it when I saw it. Johns Hopkins had it in medicine; MIT had it in engineering and technology; John Deere had it in the farm implement business. I had no magic formula or breakthrough ideas to get us there. Insurance is a mundane business. Success comes from executing the fundamentals of underwriting, claim handling, and information processing better than the competitors.

I asked for the help of my employees. Further, I told them it wasn't my dream that was important, but theirs. If our company had more people than our competitors did who were coming to work to build what they wanted to achieve, we would have a competitive advantage.

It is indisputable that we each need oxygen for a healthy physical life, but it is not so self-evident that each of us needs aspirations for a healthy interior life, no matter what position we occupy in a corporate pecking order. Winning companies in this century will not be distinguished by the creativity or grammatical perfection of their vision statement. Rather, they will be distinguished by the quality of the aspirations of their people. I encouraged local or departmental visions because it is the responsibility of every manager at every level to be mindful of the aspirational dimension of work and to provide the context for it to flourish.

To reverse a food chain descent, you need a leader who is believable and a story that gives hope. But does transformation have to begin at the top? Most people seem to think so. And certainly the probability of success is enhanced if the top people are behind any effort to transform a culture. But what if you are a mid-level manager in a firm where the works are all gummed up by dysfunctional relationships, where office politics is the name of the game, and where bureaucracy is valued more than human judgment? What if you feel the enterprise is sliding down the food chain—maybe living off a reputation earned in the past?

I started my career at the bottom and worked up the ranks. I had four employers before I signed on with Jack Adam and Hanover. During that time, I had a lot of bosses. A few were superb. A few were turkeys. I learned from both kinds. But generally, at Hanover, I was given the freedom to do my work in a way that aligned with the principles that Jack Adam and I built into the Hanover culture and that are described in this book.

To gain the freedom to put my ideas into practice, I found I had to be good at two dimensions of my job. First, I had to be able to make the case for what it was I wanted to do and how I was going to do it. Second, I had to deliver results. Neither requirement was unreasonable. Even though many bosses don't know how to support cultural change and don't have any interest in it, they do tolerate it if it is accompanied by results, as it should be.

Conversely, what is the price of going with the downhill flow? It is that inner feeling of absence, an emptiness which over time will douse the fire in your belly and change who you are. We all deserve more.

Climbing off the bottom entailed some big battles. It was important not to let bureaucracy, procedure, and tradition get in the way of doing the right thing. I sometimes saw bureaucrats—with the best of intentions, and in the name of fairness, equity, and uniformity—block wise efforts to reverse our descent down the food chain. For instance, we heard, "We can't hire good people because we can't pay them enough." Then a manager might find a person who looked good and checked out favorably. But personnel would say, "We can't pay the market wage that prevails because to do so would be unfair to everyone else." Meanwhile, the whole company was sinking because of a lack of talent. No one such decision has a fatal impact. But the accumulation of this kind of thinking leads companies to the corporate graveyard.

Our first step toward resolving this situation was to place hiring and salary authority with our line managers. After all, they were responsible for bottom-line results, and if the new hire turned out to be an overpaid turkey, they would have to face the consequences.

But the fundamental solution was in adopting a few core values to guide us in our thinking about the difficult governance issues we faced. Each value arose out of real business situations that we faced in the journey from the bottom. These values served as antibiotics for particular diseases that infected our culture.

Values are deeply held core beliefs that must be voluntarily embraced—they cannot be mandated or coerced. Good values are antidotes to inferior behavior. We live up to our values, even when it is difficult because we believe it is right to do so.

Leaders do not create values. Values are etched in the spiritual DNA of humans. The attraction of truth, the desire to love and be loved, and the appetite for freedom to become more and serve better are embedded in the nature of people. Leaders simply call forth a value from the rich history of moral wisdom accumulated over time to counter the dominant dysfunctions within the domains for which they are responsible.

For example, here's the story about how our value of localness was adopted within Hanover. In 1974, while still struggling to climb off the bottom, Hanover had the chance to buy Citizens Insurance Company, an outstanding Michigan company with a superb management team led by Roy Westran. The company had a superior ten-year track record under Roy; it was one of the top two insurance companies in Michigan; and the price was right. As we were consummating the deal, the informal conversation among the vice presidents who reported to Jack Adam began to center on "how we would run them after we owned them." I was deeply bothered. Here was a subsidiary with a track record coming into our family, and the prevailing mental model was "We own them, and therefore we'll tell them what to do"—even though we didn't have our own house in order yet, and even though the Citizens' management team knew more about the insurance marketplace in Michigan than we could ever hope to. They had excelled at building special relationships with their agents that I believed could not be transferred to a company from the East Coast.

I spoke to Jack about my concerns, and he scheduled a special meeting for senior management. All the concerns got on the table. We had a deliberate dialogue out of which emerged many of the ideas that constituted our value of localness, even though we did not get around to naming this value "localness" until a number of years later.

All our core values were born out of live business issues where inferior mental models (for example, hoarding power) were replaced by those that called for the best from our people—and we knew that people can be trusted. At the risk of being redundant, I repeat this point because I have watched executives conceive their own values and then try to sell or force them on their organization. The job of adopting values works better when people understand the disease, participate in concocting the remedy, and are free to choose their own dosage.

As the "climbing-off-the-bottom" period proceeded, we learned a lot about applying our values to business issues. Values are simple to understand and easy to remember, but learning to live up to them in the conduct of business is a lifetime's work.

Over the years, we got off the bottom of the food chain by doing hundreds of little things better. It was pick-and-shovel work. By becoming more competent at settling claims, at underwriting and pricing, and at providing our agents with better service, we just kept raising the bar for everything we did. Meanwhile, we paid a lot of attention to our purpose, visions, and emerging values.

How did our people respond? At first, only a handful reacted with genuine enthusiasm. They were the believers. More than a few were cynical. But most adopted a wait and see attitude, thinking, "This, too, will pass." As we had more success, we attracted more believers.

I don't know the exact day we climbed off the bottom of the insurance industry. But I do remember the day when we knew we were off the bottom, which was probably three years after the time we actually moved up. In 1975 the property and casualty industry suffered its worst insurance operating loss in history, with an average combined ratio of 108.2. Insurance is like golf—the lower the score, the better. So 108.2 means that for every $100 of premiums it collected, it lost $8.20 before considering investment income. But even in these tough times, Hanover bettered the industry by five-tenths of a point (107.7). It was proof that we were off the bottom.

When the insurance industry goes through an adverse cycle, many individual companies have Pavlovian reactions that spread pain to all their constituencies. Agency contracts are terminated, employees are laid off, commissions are lowered, branch offices are closed, and companies often quit entire states. These kinds of actions were undertaken by the big-name and admired companies of that time. But Hanover steered a steady course through that period of adversity, refraining from sweeping actions. Our steadiness enhanced our reputation among agents—but, more important, it did something palpable inside our employees. It was clear that we had earned our way out of our inferiority complex and that we now aspired to play at another level. The changes that drove our performance in 1975 took place in 1972, 1973, and 1974. We just didn't know how well they would work until we got the report in 1976 for the results in 1975.

SECOND STAGE: TURNING THE CORNER

Beating the industry average by five-tenths of a point was certainly better than being at the bottom, but that was not our aspiration. Just in case anyone might be tempted by complacency after our leap of improvement, Jack Adam introduced the notion of "never arriving" into our philosophy. The central tenet of "never arriving" is that the journey is more important than the destination, and that reaching one plateau is simply the beginning of an ascent to the next. It was a wise move at the right time.

The keys to turning the corner were upgrading our people, getting our philosophy out of the bottle and into practice on the front line, getting scorecards and information out so people could keep track of how they and the company were doing, and changing the structure to fit the emerging philosophy.

Upgrading Our People

A good culture—one that is generative, that uplifts people, that calls forth people's peak energy—will not cut it without talented people. But it is surprising what happens when the infections in a culture are cured and standards are raised. Much of our talent was grown from within as we changed the culture, but if we were to play at a higher level, we needed people with more talent than we had employed during our sub-par era. How did we go about acquiring them?

For me, the key in building our human talent was in telling a story about our aspirations, beliefs, and strategies with conviction and passion in a way that was totally free of exaggeration or spin. It was not a selling session but a candid explanation of who we were trying to become. When aspirations are combined with sound ideas and talked about with passion, they become contagious.

Even though we hired only a small percentage of the people we interviewed, we did try to convert everyone we talked to into becoming a Hanover fan, a carrier who would help spread the word about us in the industry. Most industries are close-knit communities, and word quickly gets around. Soon there was a buzz about us that was invaluable in recruiting employees and, particularly, agents, who are independent businesspeople.

Telling the story was half the job. It is also an art to be able to read people to the extent that you deliver a good batting average in choosing the ones who will fit productively in a values-based, vision-driven culture. No one bats a thousand in the hiring game, nor is there only one right way to do it. I will share with you my approach.

I set aside three hours for the interviews because I considered the job of ratcheting up the quality of our people to be one of my most important responsibilities. This was just as true for my twelve years as CEO as it was for my eight-plus years of service under Jack Adam.

You may think you can't afford that kind of time to interview job applicants who have already been interviewed several times. But if you have ever been involved in the pain, expense, and lost opportunity that occurs when you have had to undo a hiring mistake, you know that an extra couple of hours on the front end is inconsequential. I frequently found that people whom I was ready to dismiss after fifteen minutes of an interview often got more interesting an hour later, when I was able to explore deeper inside them. Of course, the reverse often happened as well, and that was even more important.

The ground rules of the interview process were that I had forty-five minutes to tell the story about Hanover, the candidate then had forty-five minutes to tell me about him- or herself, and the remaining hour and a half would be a freewheeling discussion about what had emerged from the first half of the conversation. This process offered some structure but also a lot of flexibility to wander down rabbit trails.

The candidates normally nominated me to go first so they could organize their stories. I would tell the Hanover story, building it around our roots, our current reality, and our vision. When we came to the candidate's story, I began by asking the candidate to "Take me through your life, from the beginning, and tell me how each period influenced your becoming who you are today."

I listened as intently as I knew how. Generally, I found the stories fascinating. Occasionally, candidates had a tendency to skip the commentary about how what they had experienced had influenced who they were today. That told me a lot about their reflective capacity and their lack of inclination to pay attention to their growth. I, of course, brought them back to the key question.

I had a series of questions to help me get a deeper understanding of who they were on the inside, such as these: If you were to do college over, what would you do differently? Tell me about the best boss you worked for (no names). Tell me about the worst boss you worked for (again, no names). Who are your heroes? Why? If you were made CEO of your company tomorrow morning, what would be the top three issues on your list? Additionally, I would share vignettes from my own life if they seemed to fit the conversation in a helpful way.

There were no right or wrong answers to these questions, nor did I try to judge them as such. I would simply let the whole conversation wash over me to give me a reading of the candidate's values, aspirations, philosophy of life, and quality of thought. I was especially trying to read the candidate's "size." I would ask myself: Is he or she big enough for the job at hand? Will the people under him look up to him? Does she grasp complexity? Does he grasp nuances? Can she see around corners? Is he mature enough to handle the tension between self and selflessness?

The "size" issue became more important as Hanover ascended to higher levels on the food chain. Our people expected more maturity and wisdom from us, and the job of leadership became larger. We began to concentrate on hiring people committed to personal growth.

We thought it was important that the process of hiring managers include at least three interviews at intervals of at least a week. It takes time to digest deep interviews and reflect on their meaning. Digestion and reflection are important steps in making sound decisions. For example, the first interview usually resulted in what I called "niggles," concerns that tugged inside me. I devoted the second interview to a candid discussion of the niggles, both the candidate's and mine.

An important step in our hiring process for managers, supervisors, and technical personnel was an evaluation by a management psychologist who understood our culture, our standards, our character, and our personality. Our psychologists were members of nearby independent professional firms, whom we chose with great care. We found the psychological evaluations to be of great benefit in helping us upgrade the quality of our staff because they were quite precise in measuring a candidate's intellectual capacity. If you have a job for which you need someone who is in the ninetieth percentile, you will soon be frustrated if you put someone in the slot who is in the eightieth percentile, even though he or she is otherwise an outstanding person. Psychologists are also quite accurate in reading a person's maturity. Most important, a psychologist who has a broad practice usually masters the art of calibrating the "size" of candidates. Over time, as our managers worked with the psychologists, their own capacity to read the interior qualities of people improved, as did their ability to mentor members of their staffs.

We had three simple ground rules for implementing the evaluation process:

1) A manager had to decide who her first choice was for the job and send that person for the psychological evaluation. Managers, not the psychologists, made the decision to hire. It was a cultural taboo to send two candidates to be evaluated to see which one looked best to the psychologist.

2) A manager could override a poor psychologist's report. Most of the times we did it, we regretted it. But there were exceptions.

3) If a manager was hiring someone who would report directly to her, the candidate also had to be interviewed by the manager's boss. As CEO, I had, at different times, from ten to thirteen people reporting directly to me, who in turn probably averaged eight people reporting directly to them. The impact of our hiring practices began to hit our front line when we got to the fourth or fifth management level because by 1991, we had 5,000 employees and 3,000 independent agents.

In addition to hiring, every manager faces situations where her responsibility to an individual who is not performing to the standard is in tension with her responsibility to the seaworthiness of her ship. Her first responsibility is to help the individual get to the standard. But if the individual will not or cannot, since the manager's most fundamental responsibility is to the whole enterprise, she must give the person a scholarship (via decent severance and counseling) to a competitor. We did not transfer anyone who failed in one department to another department.

Managers seldom flunked out of their jobs at Hanover because they didn't work hard or were not smart enough. The main reasons they flunked out were: 1) size—the job outgrew them; 2) hubris—they thought they were smarter than they were; and 3) victimology—"It's not my fault, but the rest of the world screwed us."

In looking back over my tenure as CEO, I find that one of the most fruitful decisions I made was engaging our principal psychologist, Lester Tobias. Generally, most management psychologists are competent in profiling the psychological attributes of candidates and staff. The measure of the exceptional psychologist is the number of people he helps to reach new levels of growth and maturity.

During his decade-long association with Hanover, Les had a profound influence on an unusually large number of executives. Equally important, he was a mentor's mentor to so many managers that there was a ripple effect throughout the organization. Further, Les was a valuable sounding board for me on many occasions, helping me to think through issues that were instrumental in nourishing the health of our culture.

Moving the Culture toward Maturity

By the late seventies, we had identified the diseases that infected our culture and committed to the values that transcended the virus. Our people had clear visions of what their local operations aspired to become. Personal growth was a hot topic. And the insurance industry was beginning to notice the company's financial track record and general improvement in operations.

At the time, three concerns fueled my own path on the journey to "never arriving":

1) The understanding of our values and their application was not as deep as it needed to be.

2) The passion and excitement about the emerging culture were beginning to fade as our field offices moved farther and farther away from our headquarters.

3) Operations and philosophy were practiced as two separate subjects. Our people liked our philosophy and practiced it from their own positions upward, but their practices downward often were not connected to it. It is hard to replace deeply ingrained old habits, even with better ones.

Until this point, the job of attending to Hanover's culture had been a part-time activity for Jack Adam and then myself. But both of us had full-time, regular work—it was time to get help. As so often happens when you set out to ascend to a higher plateau, synchronicity occurred in the form of meeting Lee Bollman. Lee was a protégé of Chris Argyris, a distinguished professor at The Harvard School of Business. Argyris was the father of a flock of theories about the infirmities that usually afflict conversations and the remedies needed to cure them. He demonstrated the effectiveness of his work to our senior management group by showing us the flaws in our own conversation. If we didn't fix them, we realized, we would not be able to live up to our values of merit and openness.

Lee designed a course for us called "Merit, Openness, and Localness" (or "MOL," as we called it) to help our people understand and internalize our values. Values are initially grasped intellectually, and only after discussion and reflection are they internalized and taken beyond the mind to the heart. Unless values are taken to this deeper level, they are not values but merely a list of preferences. Values serve us best when they help us resist temptation. When there is no temptation, we probably don't need to rely on values.

The course was held off-site and ran for three full days. We held highly participative discussions that were centered on live business issues. The course also contained a major segment on improving conversation skills, inquiry, and advocacy, particularly how to advocate without shutting down challenges.

This course helped establish our culture as more than Adam's and O'Brien's pet project. Ideas were tested in discussion, practiced, and found to stand on their merits. We bent over backward to keep the process free of coercion—values are only values when they are freely chosen. Intentional or unintentional coercion designed to force values on a group is counterproductive.

Demand to attend the course was so great that we decided to hire a person to head our philosophy operation. Again, synchronicity struck, this time with Tom Grimes. Tom had been an organizational development executive with a major oil company, a technology company, and a large insurance company. Soon, to meet demand, we added another organizational development specialist to Tom's staff.

As we added to our curriculum courses about thinking and relationships to supplement the ones on values and conversation, it became apparent that by offering our people lifetime learning that went beyond just job skills, the pay-off for us was enormous. These courses were key in enrolling the "whole person" in the mission of our enterprise. The MOL approach to education in corporate philosophy embedded our values deeper in the people of the organization and integrated them into our business decisions.

Looking back, if I were doing this over, I would triple the investment we made in education about our corporate philosophy. I am convinced that as long as we kept the endeavor lean and focused, the payoff would be high in further unleashing untapped potential within our people.

The Annual Visit

Once each year I visited each employee of the company. On average, I conducted two of these visits each month, January through October. The evening before my visit to the local office, I would meet its president for dinner to hear about his vision and assessment of current reality. My purpose during these visits was to help in any way I could to empower the local organization. Empowerment derives from three conditions—a shared vision, employee trust in management, and employee confidence that management trusts in them. Of these three, the last is not the least, but it is often the most neglected. Our evening over dinner was usually a relaxed affair, and the conversation traveled down many trails—not always directly.

The next day, I walked through the local office and had a brief conversation with each person. I would ask new employees for two ways that Hanover was different from their former companies—one way in which Hanover was better and one in which we were not as good. I would ask longer-term employees how we had changed since they came on board. Occasionally I would ask them what they would do differently if they were president. I learned a lot from these visits, meeting some great people at all levels while having a barrel of fun.

After talking to each employee individually, I would talk to all the employees in a group. The groups ranged in size from sixty to six hundred. In one city, we rented a nearby movie theater (they are cheap at 10 a.m.!), while in another, we rented a large tent. Each speech focused on some important aspect of our philosophy. One year, for example, I talked about Vision; another year, my topic was Advanced Maturity. I used the occasion not only to build an understanding of our philosophy, but also to promote the notion of using work to advance one's personal growth. I ended each talk with a half-hour question session.

After the talk with employees ended, I met with the local management team for an hour or two. Later I met with about a dozen or more of our agents, who were independent businessmen and not inclined to be awed by corporate titles. There never was an agenda for this meeting. Our agents never needed one. These meeting were invaluable for me. They kept me grounded and tuned in to what was happening on the front line.

Belief systems that endure have rituals. Our country has its inaugural address, a State of the Union speech, Fourth of July parades, and so on. As we built Hanover's culture, it was important to include rituals that kept the fire in our culture burning. The President's Annual Visit was such a ritual.

The Blue Books

I put a lot of work into my annual speech for employees. I knew I was constructing the philosophy that undergirded our corporate character. But sometimes I got discouraged by how rapidly the content of a speech or memo evaporated from the minds of listeners or readers. In trying to battle this "evaporation effect," we came up with the idea of publishing pamphlets of ten to fifteen pages each, which we called "Blue Books" because that was the color of their cover as well as the corporate color. In an effort to get the most results from the least work, many of my annual talks were converted to Blue Book to serve as source documents for our philosophy. If you think about it, all belief systems have source documents as well as rituals.

We expanded rapidly in the mid-eighties and had to recruit a lot of people. The Blue Books became popular recruiting tools. We learned that one of the best ways to grow believers in a company's philosophy is to give a person the job of explaining it to someone else. But this method works only if the philosophy is sound and practical.

Understanding the Rules and Knowing the Score

One exhilarating aspect of being CEO is that each month you receive a report on the performance of the company as a whole, as well as on each of its major parts, and at the end of each quarter, the reports of your competitors appear in the financial pages. You can quickly calculate how your company compares.

These reports are an enormous source of motivation. If they show good performance, the satisfaction runs deep, and the applause delights. If they show poor performance, the concern also runs deep, and the criticism hurts. It is a wonderful playing field to keep you focused and growing.

It occurred to me that if I believed this kind of feedback was so healthy for me, why not replicate it to the extent practical and have a similar environment for as many of our managers as possible? There were limits on what I could do to spread financial ownership—but a lot could be done by being innovative and generous with psychological ownership. When we were "climbing off the bottom" with a limited financial department, it took all the department had to feed the necessary financial numbers to the CEO and board of directors. As we improved the company, our reporting got better, but not good enough to take us up to another plateau.

Again, synchronicity stepped in to help us out. At the time I was looking for a CFO, a new phrase was being bandied about in the accounting profession—"creative accounting." I never saw a definition of the phrase in writing, but I sensed what it meant from how it was used—interpreting accounting rules so that unsatisfactory financial results appear less unsatisfactory than they really are. When our new CFO prospect, Joe Henry, and I were courting each other, we agreed that the financial system that ought to undergird Hanover's values-based, vision-driven culture had to be full and forthright explanation of our financial performance, formatted and explained so nonaccountants could easily understand reality. It was important that the numbers be believable to the men and women making the daily operating decisions. One of the unintended consequences of BS'ing external audiences is that the internal constituents, whom you depend on to run the company, lose faith in the numbers. They no longer trust the navigation system.

Joe Henry, working closely with John Hogan, our VP in charge of automation, and with our local company management teams, did a great job of constructing clear profit-and-loss statements and balance sheets for our more than twenty profit centers. They were formatted to be easily understood, and they provided the backup data to see what was behind the numbers. Why balance sheets? With just a profit-and-loss statement, everything disappears on December 31. Earnings and losses are absorbed into the parent company. With a balance sheet, each year becomes part of the long-term record. We wanted our managers to think long term. The introduction of local balance sheets had a pronounced impact on the thinking of our local managers.

"Understandable" and "believable" are two different things. At the time, I was interviewing a lot of people for a couple of high-level positions, and I was shocked by the number of people with our competitors at the vice president level and above who did not believe their company's numbers. When I would ask them about the operating ratios for their area of responsibility, they would refer to adjustments that were made each month by an inner circle and never explained to them in a believable manner. In their culture, it was apparent that the connection between a manager's operating decisions and financial performance was broken. In our culture, I thought it was imperative that all our people saw the connection between their decisions and actions and our financial performance. Reserve adjustments as well as allocation changes had to be explained up and down the organization. I didn't want a financial department that overfed the CEO with data and analysis and underfed line management.

One Story—the Real One—for Everyone

Each month I submitted an operating report to our board of directors. At the same time, the same report and interpretation was sent to our top 325 managers. They were expected to share it with our people. Our operating results were not always good, but they were true to the best of our knowledge. Joe Henry and his team did an outstanding job of maintaining the integrity of our numbers and of our key constituencies' trust in them.

Each quarter, our financial department prepared two sets of displays ranking the top forty companies in our industry, one by combined ratio (a proxy for underwriting profit) and the other by rate of premium growth (increase in sales). One set was for the current quarter. The other was for the most recent ten-year period. Both the long-term and the immediate present are important. These displays were exhibited in the lobbies of all our offices and published in our internal publications. They contributed to our sense of striving to ascend from one plateau to another. They were, for us, the equivalent of the league standings that major league baseball uses to keep fans informed as to how each team is doing.

Moving a culture from a top-down, command-and-control organization to one that is vision-driven and values-based takes more than coming up with a picture of "what ought to be" and a few values. There are a lot of attendant subtheories that come with command-and-control that must be rethought and attended to. For instance, under command-and-control, it makes sense to distribute information on the basis of "need to know." Why waste people's time with information that only fills out context if you are going to tell them what to do? Under command-and-control, it is logical for a manager to view his people as business servants whose main responsibility is to please him. In contrast, my interior disposition toward each individual who reported to me was, "What can I do to help you complete yourself, to be the best among your counterparts in the insurance industry?"

The formation of these interior dispositions, in a deeply authentic way, is at the heart of the leadership development needed to move our institutions toward healthier cultures. Getting managers at all levels to examine their interior assumptions is an important part of transformation. When you get a culture headed north, high-road choices become contagious. Unfortunately, when a culture is headed south, low-road choices also become contagious.

I knew that who I was as CEO was partly what I brought to the job from my first forty-six years on this earth. But I also knew that who I was as CEO was what the nature of the job brought out of me. It is easy to overestimate the first and underestimate the second. That is why we see so much hubris and why its antidote, humility, is so important.

My twelve years as CEO was a phenomenally happy experience—I was contributing and growing. But I don't think you have to be a CEO to have this kind of experience. Classroom teachers, school principals, department managers, pastors, and shopkeepers can have the same satisfaction that comes from running something in a way that pulls its people up.

Because I appreciated what the environment in the CEO's office did for me, I tried to move that environment as far throughout the company as I could. I am talking about such environmental factors as understanding the whole, knowing the context of issues, and having access to information, forums for making views known, and the authority to do one's job.

Fitting the Structure to Fit Our Philosophy

During the seventies and eighties our competitors in the insurance industry seemed to reorganize themselves almost every other year. Each time they did, it was a major distraction for their employees and agents. It was good for us.

We followed an unspoken rule. Don't change the structure of the organization until two years after the philosophy that underlies the change is internalized by the people affected by the change. That sure limited the amount of reorganization we did! For instance, two years after we internalized the value of localness, we began to take levels of management out of the organization. We went from three tiers (national, regional, and branch) to two tiers (national and local company). Also, whenever we faced a choice between increasing the span of oversight or adding a level, we had a strong bias toward the former.

In the seventies and eighties, the name of the game was "climb the ladder." But for the good of the enterprise, we were taking rungs of the ladder out. It was a considerable task at the time to convince our people to direct their energy toward horizontal growth (growing their area of responsibility) and to trust that vertical growth (climbing the ladder) would ensue. This kind of reorganization required us not only to change the structure but also to compose the mental models that were behind the changes.

✦ In our early days of climbing off the bottom, to workers in a branch it seemed as if the company was run by fear through a series of functional (not financial) audits by the key departments in the headquarters office. There were a lot of problems with this form of governance—for example, decisions were made more to pass audits than to satisfy customers and earn profits. It was not a work environment that fostered responsibility.

✦ Agents doing business with us sensed we were making decisions in anticipation of audits instead of on the basis of someone's mature judgment. This impeded the building of vital local relationships between underwriters and agents, which are at the heart of being a great underwriting company.

✦ A unit could pass the audit and still be third-rate.

✦ The audit primarily emphasized the condition of the files and not the reality of the situation.

✦ A local unit could be the best underwriter in its market, but be noted only for its clerical mishaps.

Consequently, as part of moving forward the value of localness, we took several steps:

✦ We significantly reduced the size of our headquarters staff. Less than nine percent of our people worked at headquarters. Many of our competitors, at the time, had over thirty percent of their people in the home office.

✦ Unless a local unit had a prolonged poor record, an audit was a consulting service to local management and not a checkup by the national office. As a consulting service, it was by invitation.

✦   We taught the members of our national staff consulting skills. Consultants don't get invited back unless they are seen as providing a service of value. Traditional auditors from headquarters are frequently viewed as instruments to wield power and exercise control.

Changing the underlying nature of our functional audits was just a first step in changing our structure to fit our philosophy—in this case localness.

We also tried to increase the degree to which we replicated the environment in my office and the motivation it afforded me. The board of directors was the principle source of feedback on how I was doing. Additionally, our daily listed stock price was feedback. The whole process of board governance—the preparation, the presentations, the dialogue, and the relationships—was a source of uplift and inspiration for me. The people who led our local units had a boss and a series of functional audits to let them know how they were doing—could we improve our structure to give our local management teams the same environmental advantages I was enjoying?

So we formed internal boards of directors as the overseeing body for each of our local companies (which were the equivalent to the branch offices of our competitors). Our zone vice presidents, who had each been overseeing about eight local companies, became chairmen of the local boards. The members included the president of the local company, usually one or two of his peers from another part of the country, and a couple of functional vice presidents (or managers reporting directly to them) from among the CFO or the underwriting, claim, or marketing executives. The board as a whole knew the insurance business, the company's philosophy, and our strategies. The members each had senior responsibilities of their own. Also, the process helped the vice presidents of specialized functions to acquire a deeper understanding of the business as a whole. The connectivity and the unintended consequences were now being experienced by our senior managers.

A big advantage of the internal board arrangement for governance of our local operations was the "lift-up" effect it had on the individual members of the local management team. It was exciting to watch their increased confidence from participating in the board meetings. And the growth in the breadth of their perspectives was palpable. These meetings became important rituals for our local companies, and significantly advanced psychological ownership locally. Our people really felt that they ran their own companies.

What activities that were centralized could be better done locally? It was obvious that our computer processing, which was locked into a mainframe system at the time, had economies of scale that made it not feasible to do locally. But we did think of another long-time headquarters function that we could do locally—rate setting and the attendant filings with state regulatory agencies. The local people knew the territory better, had more common ground with the players at the state regulatory agencies, and could get the filings acted on sooner in amounts closer to what they wanted. More important, the local management owned the new rates when they had to sell them to their agents. Under the old arrangement, new rates (usually higher) were something the home office "did" to them. Now, the local management team reviewed the loss data, the inflation expectations, and the competitive profiles themselves. They believed in what they were doing. Also, several of our young actuaries in headquarters transferred to local operating companies and eventually became key players for us. Meanwhile, we kept a small but excellent actuarial staff at the headquarters office, which served as a sounding board and backup when needed. The cost was more than offset by the benefits of better pricing.

There were other instances in which moving services out from the national office helped complete the self-standing nature of our local operations. A decision to do this usually came down to resolving the tension between economies of scale and the benefits of deep psychological ownership of their responsibilities by the people who get the job done.

In 1984 the industry's combined ratio broke the record again for "worst ever," at 120.5. Hanover recorded a 110.4. We beat the industry at the worst point in the cycle by 10.1, up from .5 nine years earlier. While we had been gradually turning the corner since we climbed off the bottom, we knew we had done it when we put 1984 to bed.

ON OUR WAY—UP ANOTHER MOUNTAIN

"Climbing off the Bottom" and "Turning the Corner" were accomplished by identifying the diseases that infected our culture; by adopting values that cured the diseases; by embedding these values deep into the organization; by consciously going after the best people we could find; by creating rituals and structure to keep the philosophy alive and relevant; and by maintaining reports, scorecards, and comparative standings so every employee could be a knowledgeable fan of the company. Throughout this period we were fortunate to have companies—some inside the insurance industry, but most outside—that we used as role models. Put simply, by combining good people with a healthy culture, we did what we knew we should be doing better than most of our competitors. It was more virtue than smarts—the good of the whole was put ahead of self-interest: Merit over office politics, truth over manipulation and spin (Openness), and freedom over domination (Localness).

The next mountain facing us was to significantly improve the quality of our thinking. When you run out of role models, you no longer have anyone to copy. You have to figure out the game yourself. I wasn't envisioning one, two, or three very smart people who could come up with great ideas and then tell everyone else what to do. I don't have much faith in that kind of organization. My vision was to elevate the capacity for thought in every person in Hanover for its application to the fundamental arts of insurance—underwriting, loss settlements, information processing, and selling.

While these notions about better integrating our philosophy with our business practices were percolating inside my head, another fortuitous incident influenced me. I happened to read Plato's dialogue with Glaucon, in which Plato says that until philosophers become kings, or kings take the pursuit of philosophy seriously, there will never be a conjunction between power and deep intelligence. The two temperaments—that of the rulers, who remain firm when tested by fire, and that of the philosophers, with their quickness of apprehension and largeness of soul—seldom are found in one person. But developing this combination of qualities in leaders, according to Plato, is the "smallest change" that would transform the governance of cities.

Substitute "academics" for "philosophers," "executives" for "kings," and "corporations" for "cities," and Plato had the same damn problem almost 4,000 years ago that I now was wrestling with! Even though neither Plato nor Glaucon had a solution to the problem of putting these two temperaments together, it was clear to me that segregating deep thought from business practices was an obstacle to transformation.

Once again it was synchronicity that helped us up another mountain. I was kibitzing with one of our board members, Bob McCray, about my aspiration to elevate the quality of thinking in our organization when he told me about John Beckett, a professor of management at the University of New Hampshire in Durham, who had turned Bob's son on to intellectual pursuits.

So I asked Jack Adam, who was now retired, to join me for a lunch with Beckett. We three were kindred spirits. All were contrarians with a disdain for the superficial and the irrelevant, and with a strong appetite for understanding underlying causes. Beckett told us he called his course "Thinking About Thinking." Its nickname was "Sandpaper on the Brain." It began with the history of Western thought and science, most of which Jack and I had studied in school but had forgotten. Then it moved on to Eastern thought, which was new to us. All of it made so much sense—but the conclusions were so different. How could this be? Wasn't there supposed to be one right answer?

After the lunch, I talked with Jack. He thought Beckett was solid and might contribute to accomplishing what I wanted to do in raising the quality of our thinking. So I engaged Beckett. His course was to run for thirteen weeks, every other Monday afternoon for four hours. He insisted on two weeks between sessions for the proper digestion of the ideas. The participants were the twelve people who directly reported to me, myself, and, of course, Jack Adam.

After the first three or four sessions, I thought I was going to have a mutiny on my hands. All I heard was, "What's this got to do with the insurance business?" or "What's this got to do with making money?" or "Why are we wasting a half day every other week listening to this guy?" But around the fifth week, it began to come together for all the participants. We began to understand that through our education and Western culture, we saw everything through the lens of linear analysis, that is, cause-and-effect thinking. We were educated in reductionism on the assumption that if you understood each part, you would know the whole.

Beckett taught us some of the ways Eastern thinking differs from our own. He introduced us to the concepts of unintended consequences and connectivity. We became very sensitive to these two notions, and as a result we avoided doing some dumb things while exploring linear solutions to vexing issues. This course caused us to be extra sensitive to the implications of actions we were considering—and it affected the thinking of a number of our managers. For example, one member of the senior management team told me the course was causing arguments with his wife. He and his wife used to read the newspaper and generally agree on the meaning and implications of the stories they had read. But after taking Beckett's course, he found himself frequently disagreeing with her.

In spite of a few of these unintended consequences, it was clear that the course was having a positive and profound effect on the thinking of the entire senior management team. We engaged Beckett to take the course through the ranks of the company, which required him to sacrifice the two-week interval for digestion of the ideas and compress the course into a week. It just wasn't feasible to fly people thirteen times to the course in order to accommodate the digestion interval. With reluctance, he agreed.

When Beckett retired, Tom Grimes took over teaching the course. Over several years, we ran more than 1,500 people through the course in groups of approximately fifteen. The course introduced to the company a language and mental models for achieving deeper understanding of complex issues. Both John Beckett and Tom Grimes regularly received letters from completers of the course thanking them for a "life-changing experience."

As a result of Beckett's course, we saw divergent problems more clearly and understood them better. A divergent problem consists of two opposing issues such that when one is improved, the other is made worse. For instance, it is generally agreed that since so many people have to drive to get to work, automobile insurance ought to be affordable. On the other hand, Americans value their individual rights and believe that if someone is injured as a result of someone else's negligence, the injured person should be adequately compensated for the loss. As you can see, when you improve one side, you inevitably hurt the other. You have the same kind of divergent issue when you substitute "material standard of living" and "quality of the environment" into the formula. These are the kinds of problems that vex modern society today.

A convergent problem, on the other hand, is one that can be fixed by taking a series of related steps. Fixing a flat tire, balancing a checkbook, and putting a man on the moon are all convergent problems. As a society, we are good at fixing convergent problems and not so good at fixing divergent ones. Beckett's instruction helped us to better understand our divergent problems and made us smarter in avoiding steps that would make them worse. But we remained befuddled as to how to transcend them.

Synchronicity struck again when circumstances caused my path to cross with Peter Senge almost ten years before he wrote his classic, *The Fifth Discipline*. Someone sent me a copy of a paper that

Peter and Charlie Kiefer had coauthored on "Vision." It was, in my estimation, a reinforcement of the work we had done in constructing our vision at Hanover. I asked my secretary to order 100 copies for distribution to our management. When she called to put in the order, she was asked why we wanted them. When she asked me, I said, "Why do they care? We'll pay for them." But that question and the essay itself led to a rich and rewarding friendship with Peter. We were kindred spirits and shared a deep passion about what organizational life "ought to be."

I had come to this point in my own maturation through creating a corporate culture based on traditional truths about human nature, human purpose, the role of work in human happiness, values, the moral formation of leaders, and the application of all these truths to the functioning of a corporation. It was a values, vision, and virtue approach to institutional transformation. Now, at this point in our institutional development, learning, thinking, and theory building seemed to hold the potential to take us up another mountain. Certainly, all around me the evidence was growing that the paradigms of command-and-control combined with reductionism and linear analysis were losing their fit with the times.

Peter talked to me about his research in using systems dynamics to better understand complexity. Systems dynamics is a method for looking at large, complex systems—the legal system, for instance, or the health care system or the national economy—in order to understand how the action of each player causes corresponding reactions by other players that either reinforce or block a given direction. It weighs lag times as well. My gut instinct told me that here was a tool that might enable us to better use what we had learned from Beckett to understand our business issues. Systems dynamics seemed to be a better way to get at those bedeviling divergent issues that were so tough to resolve. In other words, my idea was not to oppose systems thinking to reductionism, but rather to apply a systems approach to divergent issues and reductionism to convergent issues.

In any event, Peter invited me to be part of a series of research initiatives sponsored by the Sloan School of Management at MIT, where Peter was on the faculty. The original initiative was called New Style Management, and some of the early participants were Ray Stata, CEO and founder of Analog Devices; Shelly Buckler, executive VP of Polaroid; John Rollwagen, CEO of Cray Research; Ed Simon, CEO of Herman Miller; Arie de Geus, managing director of group planning for Royal Dutch Shell; and Jay Forrester, who was Peter's mentor at MIT and one of the original thought leaders of systems thinking.

The task facing me at Hanover was to sort through a rich menu of ideas about corporate learning and select a few that would best outfit us for our journey to the next plateau. I thought there were probably four paths that would advance the quality of our thinking or of our becoming what was fashionably called "a learning organization."

1) Clean up the culture by getting rid of crap like office politics, needless bureaucracy, spin, manipulation, and inept use of power. Replace these with an appealing vision that inspires, and with deeply embedded values that are antidotes to the low-level toxins that tend to infect institutional life. We were well on the road on this one.

2) Get good at serious conversation—what we learned from Argyris, Bolman, and Grimes.

3) Introduce systems thinking throughout the company. The Beckett course was an invaluable foundation for systems thinking, but we needed the whole company to embrace systems thinking in order to raise the quality of our thinking.

4) Use scenario planning (developed by Royal Dutch Shell) as a disciplined methodology for thinking about the future. Scenarios are not predictions but alternative paths to the future.

They are wonderful tools for helping managers think their way through changing events. Using scenarios was particularly helpful to us in thinking our way through underwriting cycles.

✧   ✧   ✧

There is a lot of fog on the journey toward transformation. As you travel, you don't always know precisely where you are or whether what you are doing is exactly right. When you write about it in retrospect, as I am doing now, it seems so much clearer and certain than it did at the time we were going through it. But the turning points, the arriving at plateaus, were always verified by external assessments of solid business performance. In 1993 McKinsey, one of the world's premier consulting firms, published an assessment of the property and liability insurance industry that covered the fifteen-year period 1978 to 1993. The McKinsey Report said:

Few industries are subject to more frequent and more powerful external forces than the property-casualty industry. Health care reform and Superfund legislation at the federal level, Proposition 103, workers compensation reform and constantly changing regulatory environments at the state level, ever more creative notions of liability emerging from our judicial system, and natural disasters—these forces, and more, continually hammer the industry and require constant attention. Add the never-ending speculation about when or whether the cycle will turn, and the short-term focus that predominates in this industry is understandable.

But these external challenges are masking a long-term trend that is fundamentally changing the industry structure: the shift in wealth and market clout from marginal underwriting companies to great underwriting companies—namely AIG, American Family, Chubb, GEICO, Gen Re, Hanover, Progressive,

PUTTING PRINCIPLES INTO PRACTICE ✧ 169

Safeco, and USAA. These are the only companies among the top 35 U.S. property-casualty carriers that have achieved an average combined ratio under 105 for the 15-year period through year-end 1993.

Most satisfying to me was that we had earned our way into this top-performing group, coming from the bottom only twenty years previously. It confirmed for me that we had been "on our way."

THE END

Two connected events that occurred in 1969 precipitated Hanover's transforming journey. In that year, State Mutual Life Assurance Company bought 51% of Hanover's outstanding stock. The balance of the stock, 49%, remained publicly held.

Later in that year, the board of directors, now controlled by State Mutual affiliated directors, elected Jack Adam as its president and CEO, thus providing the original impetus for our transforming journey. For twenty-two years, during the journey and under the philosophy described in this book, Hanover operated as an independent, freestanding enterprise with our own board of directors and public stockholders.

Under this arrangement our market capitalization had grown from $120 million to $840 million and our sales from $115 million to $1.6 billion. Our profits by the late eighties and early nineties were accounting for seventy percent of State Mutual's earnings. The tail was wagging the dog.

In October 1991, I received a shocking call from the CEO of State Mutual, Jack O'Brien (no relation), who informed me that he wished to add six State Mutual people to our board as part of a reorganization that would result in SMA taking over Hanover (SMA had been buying more Hanover stock and now controlled 57%). He asked for my cooperation in adding the directors so as to effect the change in the relationship between our two companies. When I asked to him to elaborate on the implications for Hanover, I found his answers vague and unpersuasive.

There was no question in my mind as to who held the power and control—owning 57% of the stock outweighed owning 43%. Nevertheless, I opposed the move because incompatible cultures are a principle cause of failed acquisitions and mergers. Hanover's culture, as it had evolved through 1991, was based on our values and carefully cultivated local visions. State Mutual's culture, at the time, was a paternalistic version of the traditional command-and-control style. I knew our cultures would not mesh.

Furthermore, even though our financial performance had been outstanding, I believed our best years were ahead of us, if we were allowed to continue operating as an independent entity.

I thought there was, at best, a small probability that I could convince the directors of my case, even though seven of the twelve had State Mutual affiliations. I failed. Power (57%) trumped Merit (43%) in my eyes. I gave notice of my retirement on the day following the fateful board meeting. I knew I could not lead what I did not believe in.

Many people have offered me consolation over this turn of events. While I appreciate the generous sentiments behind these kind expressions, I have never felt in need of consolation. Why?

All secular institutions eventually die. It turned out that in 1991, as we were then constituted, it was our turn. We did so honorably. The more penetrating question is: "What was Hanover's contribution to the human endeavor, particularly over our twenty-two-year transformation journey?" I feel in my heart that it was pretty damn good.

Our people had an opportunity to learn and mature. Most that I knew, did.

We earned good returns for our investors. In 1969 the stock was $4 per share. In 1991 it was $39 per share.

And, since at the time the prevailing command-and-control paradigm for corporate governance was becoming increasingly obsolete, we had the incubating circumstances that allowed us to conceptualize and practice a body of ideas that might be a better model for governing business enterprises in the future. The old paradigm was highly effective in producing goods and services, but that productivity was often at the expense of an uplifting and fulfilling work life. I believe we contributed to the exploration of how to integrate creation of wealth and human fulfillment in a corporate setting.

AFTERWORD

U nder new leadership, State Mutual Life Insurance changed its name to Allmerica in 1992. The Hanover Insurance Company was included under this new holding company.

In 2001–2002, Allmerica's (i.e., State Mutual's) life insurance and investment services ran into operating difficulty because many of its variable products were linked to investment portfolios. The decline in the stock market made it difficult for Allmerica to meet the guaranteed provisions in their variable annuity products. Hanover's property and casualty insurance business generated a significant portion of Allmerica's earnings.

By 2005, what was left of Allmerica's life insurance and investment services was sold off. Hanover's property and casualty business remained. That same year, the company changed its identity back to The Hanover to leverage the name's reputation for a company that is tried and true.

ABOUT THE AUTHOR

Bill O'Brien was a man inspired by faith and reason. He believed that a career was an opportunity to find a purposeful and significant life and to contribute to the well-being of others.

But he saw that large organizations often turned young graduates full of ideals and energy into empty shells. Bill's Jesuit education (Fordham 1954) provided the context for his thinking. And as he contemplated a remedy for this fundamental flaw in organizations, he decided that the underlying problem hinged on virtue.

Bill developed an open system of management that sought to empower employees by respecting their dignity and including them in the decision-making process.

Between 1979 and 1991, when Bill was the president and chief executive officer of Hanover Insurance, the firm rose from the bottom of the insurance heap to the top. By1994, Hanover was "one of the top 10 underwriting companies," according to a McKinsey and Company report released that year.

Bill was a founding member of the board of governors of the MIT Center for Organizational Learning and was a founding partner of Generon Consulting. He died in 2002.